The Book of the Dead

(VOLUME 1)

Reading & Answer Book

ISBN-13: 978-1518850172

ISBN-10: 1518850170

http://arkpublishing.co.uk

Kemet Scribe

Bernard Paul Badham

‘The beginning of utterances (Chapters) of coming forth by day, the praises and recitations

of coming forth and going into the Necropolis which is beneficial in the Beautiful West

to be spoken on the day of burial going in and after coming out’

The Book of the Dead

'The Spells of Coming Forth by Day'

The Book of the Dead is an ancient Egyptian funerary text, used from the beginning of the New Kingdom (around 1550 BCE) to around 50 BCE. The original Egyptian name for the text, transliterated **rw nw prt m hrw**:

'The Spells of Coming Forth by Day'

Another translation would be 'Book of emerging forth into the Light.' 'Book' is the closest term to describe the loose collection of texts consisting of a number of magic spells intended to assist a dead person's journey through the Duat, or underworld, and into the afterlife and written by many priests over a period of about 1000 years.

The Book of the Dead was part of a tradition of funerary texts which includes the earlier Pyramid Texts and Coffin Texts, which were painted onto objects, not papyrus. Some of the spells included were drawn from these older works and date to the 3rd millennium BCE. Other spells were composed later in Egyptian history, dating to the Third Intermediate Period (11th to 7th centuries BC). A number of the spells which made up the Book continued to be inscribed on tomb walls and sarcophagi, as had always been the spells from which they originated. The Book of the Dead was placed in the coffin or burial chamber of the deceased.

There was no single or canonical Book of the Dead. The surviving papyri contain a varying selection of religious and magical texts and vary considerably in their illustration. Some people seem to have commissioned their own copies of the Book of the Dead, perhaps choosing the spells they thought most vital in their own progression to the afterlife. The Book of the Dead was most commonly written in hieroglyphic or hieratic script on a papyrus scroll, and often illustrated with vignettes depicting the deceased and their journey into the afterlife.

The following text for translation comes from a papyrus of the Book of the Dead belonging to a kings's scribe named, Anwy:

The Papyrus of the King's Scribe, Anwy

The papyrus of Anwy (Any) was found at Thebes and was purchased by the British Museum in 1888. It measures 78 feet by 1 foot 3 inches and is the longest papyrus of the Theban Period. It is made up of 6 indivual parts. It contains a number of chapters of the Book of the Dead, mostly accompanied by illustrations. The titles of the chapters in the papyrus are written in red. In the following texts a phonetic (grey) translation of the hieroglyphs is provided to aid word identification in the Student Work Book and in the Reading & Answer Book, an English transliteration and a full literal translation is given for reading and study. This work is taken from the Papyrus of Anwy and other sources to complete the utterances of the Book of the Dead.

The Four Sons of Horus

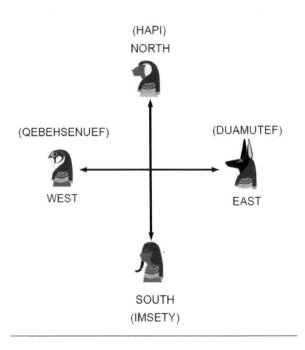

'As for the tribunal which is behind Osiris, Imsety, Hapy, Duamutef and Qebehsenuef, it is these who are behind the Great Bear (constellation Ursa Major) in the northern sky'
Book of the Dead Chapter 17 Plate 9

Guideline Example of Trasliteration and Transalation:

1. Identify words using a red pen (as the ancient scribes): phonograms usually start a word and determinatives end the word, as does the single, dual and plural strokes or the feminine ending **t** or the abstract sign of a papyrus scroll.

2. Write out the phonetic transliteration (how it sounds in ancient Egyptian minus the vowels).

Golden Rule: transliterate in groups of a maximum of three words, the word groups oftern start with a preposition such as: **r, n, m** 'to, for, in' etc and end with a suffix pronoun, such as: **.f** '.he'

This is done for you in light grey, but still confirm.

3. Using a hieroglyphic dictionary* write out the literal translation of each word with alternative meanings - maintain the same word order.

4. Put into English word order - this step may be ommitted depending on the difficulty of the text.

5. Write out the full English translation:

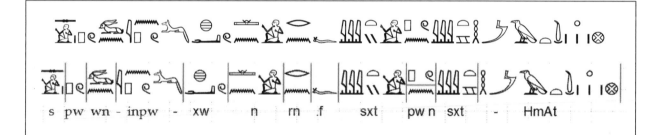

s pw, wn-inpw-xw.n, rn.f, sxty pw, n sxt-HmAt
man this, Wen-Inpu-Khu-en, name.his, peasant this, of Sekhet-Hemat (Wadi Natron)
this man Wen-Inpu-Khu-en this peasant of Wadi-Natron
'This man's name is Khu-en-wen-Inpu, he was a peasant of Wadi Natron.'

* *Sign List & Vocabulary Extended Edition - Learning to Read Hieroglyphs and Ancient Egyptian Art* by Bernard Paul Badham ISBN-10: 1508549990 ISBN-13: 978-1508549994 280 pages, 4000 entries.

THE TEXTS

PLATE 1: Hymn to the Sun god Ra

dwA ra, xft wbn.f, m Axt iAbt, nt pt

worhip Ra, when rises.he, in horizon eastern, of heaven

'Worhsip Ra when he rises in the eastern horizon of heaven'

---

in wsir sS, Htp-nTr, n nTrw nbw, Anwy

by Orisis Scribe, holy-offering, of gods all, Anwy

'by the Osiris Scribe of divine offerings of all the gods, Anwy'

Dd.f, inD-Hr.k, ii.ti, m xpri, xpri, m qmA nTrw

says.he, hail-to.you, come.you, as Khepri, Khepri as create/beget gods

'he says, Hail to you, one who comes as Khepri, Khepri who begat the gods'

xa.k, wbn.k, psd* mwt.k, xa.ti, m nsw nTrwt

rise.you, shine.you, back mother.your, appear-in-glory.you, as king gods

**'you rise, you shine, on the back of your mother (the sky)
and you appear in glory as the king of the gods'**

iry n.k, mwt nwt, awy.s, m irt, nyny sSp.tw

do to.you, mother Nut, arms-dual, as act, greeting, receive.you

'Your mother Nut will do for you, two-arms*, as an act of greeting, receives you'

* An act of greeting as represented by the man determinative with two raised arms

mAnw, m Htp, Hpt.tw, mAat r tri, di.f, Xw

western-mountain in peace, embraces.you, Maat at seasons-dual, gives.he, power-of-god

'the Western (Manu) Mountain, Maat embraces you at all seasons. May you give glory'

wsr, m mAa-xrw, prt, m bA anxy, r mAA

power, as true-voice, come-forth, as soul living, to see

'and power and as True of Voice come forth as a living soul to see'

Hrw-Axwty, n kA, n wsir sS, Anwy, mAa-xrw, xr wsir

Heru-Akhety (Horus-Two Horizons), for.ka, of Osiris Scribe, Anwy, true-voice, under Osiris

**'Heru-Akhety (Horus of the Two Horizons), for the ka of Osiris Scribe,
Anwy, True of Voice, under Osiris'**

Dd.f, i nTrw nbw, Hwt-bA, wDaw pt tA

says.he, hail/O! gods all, temple-ba, judge heaven earth

'he says, Hail all gods of the Soul-Temple who judge heaven and earth in'

mxAt, di-di.w kAw DfAw, tA-tw-nn, wa ir
balance, gives ka/food provision, Ta-tw-enen, sole-one doer/maker
'the balance, who gives food and provisions, Ta-tu-enen, sole one, maker'

Ta-tw-enen: Tatenen (also Ta-tenen, Tatjenen, Tathenen, Tanen, Tenen, Tanenu, and Tanuu) was the god of the primordial mound in ancient Egyptian religion. His name means risen land or exalted earth, as well as referring to the silt of the Nile. As a primeval chthonic (inhabiting the Underworld) deity, Tatenen was identified with creation.

tA-tw-nn 'land-you-inert, land-you-primeval-waters (Nun)' Both Tatenen and Ptah were Memphite gods. Tatenen was the more ancient god, combined in the Old Kingdom with Ptah as Ptah-Tatenen, in their capacity as creator gods. By the Nineteenth dynasty Ptah-Tatenen is his sole form, and he is worshiped as royal creator god. Ptah-Tatenen can be seen as father of the Ogdoad of Hermopolis, the eight gods who themselves embody the primeval elements from before creation.

tmw, psDt, rsy mHtt, imntt iAbtt
all-people, divine-ennead, sorthern, northern, western, eastern
'of all mankind the divine Ennead of the South and North and the West and East'

𓄿𓅱𓃀𓅃𓀜 𓂝𓇳𓇿𓀭𓊃𓏥𓆓𓋹𓍑𓋴
imi iAw, n ra, nb pt itiy, anx wDA snb
give praise, to Ra, lord heaven, sovereign, life prosperity health
'give praise to Ra, Lord of Heaven, the Sovereign, Life, Prosperity, Health'

𓁹𓊹𓊹𓊹𓇼𓏤𓅱𓄿𓀠𓋴𓅓𓁹𓏤𓆑𓄤𓅓𓈍𓆑𓅓
iri nTrw, dwA.tnw, sw, m irw.f, nfr, m xa.f, m
made gods, worship.you, him, in shape/form.his, good, in appearance.his, in
'who begat the gods, worship him in his goodly form, in his glorious appearance in'

Ra's Solar Bark:

𓊛 , 𓅐𓊛 , 𓅐𓊛 , **mandt** literally the 'Safe Boat'; 'the morning ark of the sun god, Ra'

𓊢𓂧 **aD** 'be safe'

𓅐𓊛 , 𓅐𓊛 **msktt** 'night boat, solar bark of Ra'

𓊃𓏤 **ski** 'wipe, wipe out, wipe away'

mandt, dwA.tw, Hrw, dwA.tw, Xrw
mandet-boat, worship.you, those-aove, worship.you,those below
'the Day-Bark, may those above worship you and those below worship you'

(hieroglyphs)
sS n.k, DHwty, mAat, mnt-ra nb, xft.k, rdiw
write to.you, Djhwty, Maat, day every, enemy-serpent.your given
'may Djhuty (Thoth) and Maat write to you every day, your serpent enemy given'

(hieroglyphs)
n sDt, sbiw xr, awy.f, qAsw, nHm, n
to flame, rebel-serpent fallen, arms.his, bonds, take-away/rescue of
'over to the flame, the rebel serpent has fallen, his arms bound, taken by'

ra nmtt.f, msw bdS, nn wn.sn

Ra movements/actions/procedure.his, sons become exhausted/impotent, not exist/be.them

'Ra his movements, the evil children have become weak and non-existent.'

Hwt sr, m Hb, xrw nhm, m st-wrt

temple prince, in Heb-festival, sound shout/thunder in dwelling-place-great

**'The Temple of the Prince is in Heb-Festival
and the sound of thunder is in the Great Dwelling Place,'**

---

nTrw m hai, mA.n.snw, ra m xaa.f

gods in joy, see.of.they, Ra in appearance.his

'the gods are in joy, when they see Ra in his glorious appearance'

stwt.f, Hr baH tAw, wDA Hm, nTr pn, Sps

rays-of-sun.his, upon inundate lands, go/proceed majesty, god this noble

'his rays of light inundating the lands, the majesty of this noble god proceeds'

Xnm n.f, tA n mAnw, HD-tA, r mst.f, hrw nb

enter/unite to.he, land on Manu (Western Mountain), bright-land (dawn), at birth.his day every

'and enters the Western Mountain (sun set)
and brightens the land at his birth every day (dawn)'

pH.n.f, r a.f, n sf, Htp.k, n.i, mA.i, nfrw.k

arrived/attain.of.he, to state/condition.his, of yesterday, peace.you, to.me, see.i, beauty.your

'he attained his state of yesterday, may you be at peace with me, may I see your beauty'

wDA.i, tp tA, Hw.i, aAw, bHn.i, sbiw

go/travel.i, on earth, smite.i, donkey, drive-off.i, rebel-serpent

'may I proceed upon the earth, may I smite the ass, may I drive off the rebel serpent'

s-Htm.n.i, aApp, m At.f, mA.n, AbDw sp.f, xpr

make-destroy.of.i, Aapep, in moment.his, see.of, Abedju-fish time.his, existence

'may I make destroyed the Aapep serpent at his moment,
may I see the Abedju fish in his time of being'

int.s, int m mr.s, mA.n.i, Hr m iry-Hmw

inet-fish.it , inet-boat in water-way.it, seen.of.i, Horus relating-to-steering-oar (helmsman)

'I have seen the Inet-fish and the Inet-boat in its water way, Horus as helmsman'

DHwty mAat, Hr awy.f, sSp.n HAtw, m sktt, pHwytt m aDtt

Djhuty Maat, upon hands.his, taken.of front (prow-ship),
in the sektet-day-boat, stern in adjetet-night-boat

**'with Djhwty and Maat at his side, I have taken the hold of the prow of the Sektet Night Bark
and the stern in the Adjetet Day Bark'**

gives.he, mAA iTn, dgg iaH, nn iabw, ra nb

he gives see Aten, to-look-at/behold IaH, not ceasing, day every

'may he grant to see the Aten (sun disk) and behold the Moon God, Iah, not ceasing every day'

pr bA, stwt.tw, r bw nb, mrr.f

come-out soul, travel.one, to place every, wish.it

'may my ba-soul come out to travel every place it wishes'

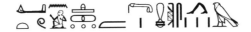

nist rn.i, gm.f, m xt wdb, xtw

call-out name.my, find.it, in board offerings

'may my name be called out, may it be found on the board of offering things'

---

di.tw.i, Htpw, m-bAH, mi Smsw Hrw

give.one.i, food/bread-offerings, before/presence, like followers Horus

'may bread offerings be given for me in the Presence, like the followers of Horus'

---

iryt.tw n.i, ist m wiA hrw, DA nTr

made.of for.me, seat in sacred-bark day, ferry-across god

'may it be made for me a place in the sacred Day Bark, when it I ferries across the god'

sSp,i, m-bAH wsir, m tA, n mAa-xrw, n kA, n wsir Anwy

receive.me, in-presence Osiris, in land, of true-voice, for ka, of Osiris Anwy

'may I be received into the presence of Osiris,
in the land of True-Voice, for the ka of Osiris Anwy'

Related Writings - British Museum Papyrus 10471

dwA ra, in sw sS, imy-r mSa, nxt

worship Ra by the king's scribe, overseer army, Nakhet

'adoration of Ra by the Overseer of the Army, Nakhet'

Dd.f, inD Hr.k, Ax-ti, spd tmw-Hrw-Axty

says.he, hail to.you, glorious.one, effective Temu-Herw-Khety

'he says, hail to you, the glorious and effective one, Temu-Heru-Khety'

iw.k, xawt m Axt, nt pt, i n.k, m rw, n Hr nbw

behold.you, rise-in-glory, in horizon of heaven, O!/shout to.you, from mouth, upon-all-people

**'behold you rise in glory in the horizon of heaven,
hail to you from the mouths of all the people'**

---

nfr.ti, rnp tr.ti, m itn, m Xnw, hand mother.your, Ht-Hr

'beautiful one, young years.one, in/as Aten, from within, hand mother.your, Hwt-Her

'beautiful one, becoming young as the Aten, from within the hand of your mother, Hat-Hor'

---

xa irk, m st nbt, ib nb, Aw n DtA

rise but/now, in place every, heart every, long-time for ever

'rise now, in every place, in every heart, for a long time, forever'

iw n.k, itrty m ks, di.snw, i n wbn.k

come to.you, chapels-two with bow-down, give.they, hail for rise-shine-appear.your

'come to you the two chapels with homage, they give hail for your shining apearance'

---

xaty m Axt, nt pt, stwt.k, tAwy mfkAt

rise in horizon of land, shoot.you two-lands turquoise

'your rising in the horizon of the land, you shed the two lands with turquoise (green light)'

---

ra pw, Hrw Axty, pA Hwn nTrty, iwa HH

Ra this-it-is, Horus horizon, the young-man/child-dual, inherit eternity

'Ra this it is Heru-Herakhety, the divine young child heir of eternity'

[hieroglyphs]
wtwt sw, msw sw Dsf, swtn tA pn, HqA dwAt
begat him, birth him him-self, king land this, prince underworld
'he begat and gave birth to himself, this king of earth, prince of the Duat (Underworld)'

[hieroglyphs]
Hr-tp DAtwt, iwgrt, prt m mw, stA sw, m nw
chief estates, realm-dead, come-forth from water, drag/draw him, from Nun
'chief of the estates of the Iugeret (Realm of the Dead), coming forth from the Water, drawing himself from Nu (Nun, god, the waters of chaos)'

[hieroglyphs]
rn(n) sw, s-Dr msTw.f, nTr anx, nb mrt
bring-up/nurse him, make-consecrated/sanctified offspring.his, god life, lord love
'nurse himself, making sanctified his offspring, god of life, lord of love'

anx Hr-nbw, psd/psD.k, xa.ti, m nswt nTrw

live people all, shine.you, crowned.one, as king gods

'all people live when you shine, crowned one, king of the gods'

---

ir.n, nwt, nyny n Hr.k, Hpt.tw mAat, r tri nb

do.of, Nut, greetings to upon.you, embrace.you Maat, at season every

'may the goddess Nut make greetings to you and Maat embrace you at every season'

Hai.n.k, imy-xt.k, dhn.snw, Hr tA, m-xsf.k

rejoicing to.you, those-who-following-after.you, bow-down.they, upon earth, at-approach-in-meeting.you

**'rejoicing to you, those who are following after you,
they bow down upon the earth at the approach of meeting you'**

𓎟 𓏏 𓎟 𓇾 𓇓𓏏 𓐙𓂝𓏏 𓎟 𓎛𓎛 𓋾𓈎𓈖 𓇓𓏏 𓊹𓊹𓊹 𓎟

nb pt, nb tA, nswt mAat, nb HH, HqA DtA, iTy nTrw nb

lord heaven, lord land, king truth, lord eternity, sovereign gods all

**'lord of heaven, lord of earth, king of righteousness,
lord of eternity, sovereign ruler of all the gods'**

𓊹 𓋹 𓁹 𓎛𓎛 𓐙𓂝 𓇯 𓋴𓏠𓈖 𓇓 𓅓 𓄡𓈖𓈖𓏏𓋴

nTr anx, ir HH, qmA pt, s-mn sw, m Xnnw.s

god life, maker eternity, creator heaven, made-established him, from within.it

'god of life, maker of eternity, creator of heaven, made established by him from within it'

𓋴𓊪𓋴𓆓𓏏 𓊹𓊹𓊹 𓎛𓈖𓅱 𓈖 𓅱𓃀𓈖𓎡 𓇾 𓅓 𓂋𓈝𓏏 𓈖 𓌳𓄿 𓇓𓏏𓅱𓏏𓎡

psDt nTrw, hnw n wbn.k, tA m rSwt, n mAA stwt.k

Pesedjet gods, jubilation/praise, rise/shine/appear.you, land in rejoicing, for seeing rays.your

**'the Pesedet (Nine) gods are in jubilation at your glorious appearance,
the earth is in rejoicing for seeing your sunshine rays '**

pr pat, m Hayw, r mAA nfrw.k, ra nb

come-out patricians/ancestors, in hails, to see beauties, day every

'the ancestors come out in shouts of joy to see your beauties every day'

DA.k, Hrt pt tA, ra nb, s-wDA.ti, n mwt.k, nwt

ferry-across.you, over heaven earth, day every, made-prosperous.one, of mother.your, Nut

'you ferry across over heaven and earth every day, made properous by your mother, Nut'

---

nmi.k, Hrt, ib.k Aw, mr n Ds-Ds, xpr m Htp

travel/traverse.you, sky/heaven, heart.your, long, pool of Dsds, become as satisfied

'you traverse the heavens, your heart is happy, the Pool of Knives has become satisfied'

sbi xr, awy.fy, qAsw, Hsq n dmt, Ts.f
rebel-serpent fallen, hands-dual.his, bonds, cut-off of knife, vertebra.his
'the Rebel Serpent has fallen, his two hands are bound, the knife cuts asunder his vertebrae'

wn ra, m mAa nfr, sktt sk.n.s, pH.sy
exist Ra, in rightous beautiful, night-bark draw.of.it, arrive.it
'Ra exists in beautiful rightousness, the Sektet-Night-Bark it draws on, it arrives'

sTA.tw, rsy mHty, imntt iAbtt, dwA.k
draw/drag.one, south north, west east, upon worship.you
'draws one, south and north, west and east, to worship you'

pAwty tA, xpr Dsf, snsy.tw, ist Hna nb-hwt

primaeval-god/man-of-ancient-family earth, creat himself, worship.you, Isis Neb-hwt

**'O primaeval god of the earth, the creator of himself,
Isis and Neb-hwt (Nephthys) worship you'**

---

s-xay.tw, m wiA pwy, awy.snw, m sAw, HA-tp.k

cause-to-appear (a god or king).you, in boat that, hands-dual.their,
in protection, behind (back-head).you

'you cause to appear in that boat, their hands in protection behind you'

Sms.tw, bAw iAbtyw, hnnw n.k, bAw imntyw

follow.you, souls easterners, praise to.you, souls westerners

'follow you the souls of the Easterners, praise to you the souls of the Westerners'

Hq.k, nTrw nbw, sSp.k, Aw-ib, m Xn kAri.k

rule.you, gods all, receive.you, long-heart, in interior shrine.your

'you rule all gods, you receive happiness inside your shrine'

---

nik isp n xt, ib.k, Aw n DtA, ip.tw, mwt.k, nwt n it nw

evil-doer judge of fire, heart.your, happy for eternity, take-heed-of-you,
mother.your to father.your, Nu

**'the evil doer is judged by fire, your heart is happy forever,
take heed you of your mother Nut, to your father, Nu'**

PLATE 2: Hymn to Awsir (Osiris)

dwA wsir, wn-nfr, nTr aA, Hr-ib, AbDw, nsw HH, nb DtA, sb(b)i HH

worship Osiris, Wen-nefer (exist-beauty), god great, upon-middle, Abydos,
king eternity, lord forever, traversing million-years

'Worship Awesir (Osiris), Wen-nefer, the great god within Abydos, king of eternity and lord of everlasting, traversing millions of years'

m aHa.f, sA tp, n xt nwt, wtt n sb/gb, rpat nb, wrrt

in life-time.his, son elder, of womb Nut, begotten of Seb/Geb,
hereditary-prince lord, crown (red and white)

'in his lifetime, eldest son of the womb of Nut, begotten of Seb (Geb), Hereditary Prince, Lord of the Ureret Crown (red and white dual crown of Upper and Lower Egypt)'

Osiris (Ausir, Asiri or Ausar), was an Egyptian god, usually identified as the god of the afterlife, the underworld and the dead. He was classically depicted as a green-skinned man with a pharaoh's beard, partially mummy-wrapped at the legs, wearing a distinctive crown with two large ostrich feathers at either side, and holding a symbolic crook and flail. Osiris was at times considered the oldest son of the earth god Geb, though other sources state his father is the sun-god Ra and the sky goddess Nut, as well as being brother and husband of Isis, with Horus being considered his posthumously begotten son. He was also associated with the epithet Khenti-Amentiu, meaning 'Foremost of the Westerners,' a reference to his kingship in the land of the dead.

28

qAi HDt, iTy nTrw, rmT, sSp.n.f, HqAt nxAxA, iAt itw.f

exalted white-crown, sovereign gods, mankind, receive.of.him, crook flail, office fathers.his

**'exalted the Hedjet (White Crown), sovereign of the gods and mankind,
he receives the crook sceptre and flail, the office of his fathers'**

Aw-ib.k, nty m smyt, sA Hrw, mn Hr nst.k

long-heart.your, which in necropolis, son Horus, established upon throne.your

**'happy is your heart which is in the Necropolis, your son, Horus,
established upon your throne'**

iw.k, xa.ti, m nb Ddw, m HqA imy AbDw

are.you, crowned.one, as lord Djedu, as ruler who-is-in Abydos

'you are crowned as lord of Djedu (Busiris), as ruler who is in Abydos'

waD n.k, tA-wy, m mAa-xrw, m-bAH, a nbr-Dr-t

flourish for.you, two-lands, in true-voice, before, hand Neber-Djer-t

**'the Two Lands flourish for you in Vindication (True of Voice),
before the hand of Neber-Djeret'**

nbr-Dr-t   literally: 'Lord to the End'

stA n.f, nty nn xpr, m rn.f, tA-Hr-stA-n.f

draw/drag/flow to.him, that/which/who? not become, in name.his, land-face-ushered-to-him

**'ushered to him that which has not yet become (all that exists) in his name,
Ta-her-seta-en-ef (Those upon the earth that are drawn to him)'**

sk n.f, tAwy m mAa-xrw, m rn.f, pwy n skr

tow/marshal to.him, two-lands in true-voice, in name.his, that of Seker

'the Two Lands are marshalled to him vindication (True of Voice) in his name, that of Seker'

[hieroglyphs]
wsr.f, Aw, aA snD, m rn.f, pwy n wsir
power.his, long, great fear, in name.his, that of Osiris
'his power is far reaching, great in fear is his name, that of Osiris'

[hieroglyphs]
wntt.f, Hnty HH, m rn-f, wn-nfr, inD-Hr.k, nswtyw, nb n nbw
exists.he, two-ends-of-time eternity, in name.his, Wen-nefer, hail-to.you king of kings, lord of lords
'he exists the two ends of time forever in his name, Wen-nefer, hail to you, king of kings and lord of lords'

[hieroglyphs]
HqA HqAw, iTit tAwy, m xt nwt, HqA.n.f, tAw igrt
prince princes, take-possession-of two-lands, in womb Nut, ruled.of.he, lands realm-of-the-dead
'prince of princes who took possession of the Two Lands, in Nut's womb he ruled the lands of the realm of the dead'

Dam Hatw, xsbd tp, mfkAt Hr-tp, awy.fy

fine-gold limbs, blue head, turquoise upon arms

'fine gold limbs, blue of head, turquoise upon his arms'

---

iwn HH, wsxt Snbt, nfr Hr, imy tA Dsr

pillar millions, broad breast, beautiful face, who-is-in land sacred

'Pillar of Millions, broad of breath, beautiful of face, who is in the Sacred Land'

---

rdi.k, Ax m pt, wsr m tA, mAa-xrw m nTr-Xrt, xd r Ddw

give.you, glory in heaven, power on earth, true-voice in god-domain, fair-down-stream to Djedu

'may you give glory in heaven, power on earth, vindication in the Necropolis, sailing downstream to Djedu (Busiris)'

m bA anx, xnty r AbDw m bnnw aq-pr

as soul living, sail-upstream to Abydos, as Bennu-Bird, in-out

'as a living soul, sailing upstream to Abydos as the Bennu Bird (Phoenix), going in and coming out'

---

nn Sna.tw, Hr sbA nbw, n dwAt

not turn-back/hinderance.you, at pylons all, of Duat

'without you being hindered at the pylon gates of the Duat (Underworld)'

---

iw rdi.tw, n.(i), tAw, m pr qbH, Htpw m iwnnw

behold given.one to.me, bread, in house cool, offerings in Iunnu

'Behold, may there be given to me bread from the House of Cool Water and offerings from Iunnu (Heliopolis)

sAH mn, m sxt-irwy, it bdt, im.f, n kA n Awsir sS, anwy

toes established, in field-reeds, barley emmer, in.it, for ka of Osiris scibe, Anwy

'toes established in the Field of Reeds, and barley and emmer wheat in it,
for the ka of Osiris Scribe, Anwy'

Weighing of the Heart Ceremony

(PLATE 3)

Chapter for not letting Anwy's heart create opposition against him in the God's Domain

Upper Register Gods: Right to Left

Ra-Horus-Akhety, Atum, Shu, Tefnut, Geb, Nut, Horus, Hathor, Sia and Hu

1. Ra-Heru-Akhety

Seated god in front of offering table with the head of a falcon and sun disk,
holding the Was-sceptre of power:

ra-Hrw-Axty, nTr nfr, Hr-ib, wiA.f
Ra-Heru-Akhety, god good, upon-heart, sacred-bark.his
'Ra-Heru-Akhety (Ra-Horus of the Two Horizons), the good god in the midst of his Sacred Bark'

2. Atum: Seated bearded god wearing the white and red crown of Upper
and Lower Egypt holding the was-sceptre:

𓏏𓅓𓏭
tmw
'Atum, the creator god of completeness'

3. Shu: Seated bearded god wearing the shu-feather of Truth holding the was-sceptre.

𓏏𓅱𓇳
Sw
'Shu, god of the Air/Dryness'

4. Tefnut: Seated god with the head of a falcon and sun disk,
holding the Was-sceptre of power:

𓏏𓆑𓄿𓈖𓏏
tf-nwt, nbwt-sxt-nt
Tef-nut (that-water), lady-field-Neith (goddess of war and hunting)
'Tef-nut, Nebut-Sekhet-Neith'

5. Geb: Seated bearded god with human head holding the Was-sceptre of power:

gb
'Geb (the earth god of the Ennead)'

6. Nut: Seated goddess with human head, holding the Was-sceptre of power:

nwt nb pt
'Nut, Lady of Heaven'

7. Isis and 8. Nephthys: Seated goddess with the throne glyph upon her head, **Isis**, next to another seated goddess with the **neb-hwt** glyphs upon her head, both hold the was-sceptre of power.

ist, nb-hwt
Isis,   Nephthys (Lady of theTemple)'
'Isis and Nephthys'

9. Horus: Seated god with falcon head holding the was-sceptre of power

𓅃 𓎤 𓏤
Hrw nTr aA
Horus god great
'Horus, the Great God'

10. Hathor

𓉗 𓎛 𓏏 𓅓
Hwt-Hr, nbt imntt
Hat-Hor (Temple-Horus), lady west
'Hat-Hor, Lady of the West'

10. Hu and 11. Sia

𓏎 𓅆   𓋴 𓅆
Hw   siA
authoratative-utterance perception/knowledge/interlect
'Hu and Sia'

Ddw in, Awsir sS Anwy, Dd.f, ib.i n mwt, sp-sn, HAty.i, n xprw

words by, Osiris scribe Anwy, says.he, heart.my of mother, repeat-twice, heart.my shape-being

'Words by Osiris Scrie, Anwy, he says, my heart of my mother, my heart of my mother, my heart of forms of being'

m aHa, r.i, mtr, m xsf, r.i, m DADAt

not stand, against.me, testify-concerning, not opposed, to.me, in magistrates

'do not stand against me in the tribunal, do not be opposed to me with the magistrates'

m irt, rq.k, r.i, m-bAH, iry mxAt, ntk kA.i, imi Xt.i

not do, turn-aside/defy, to.me, in presence, keeper balance, you ka.my, within body.my

'do not be opposed to me in the presence of the Keeper of the Balance, you are my ka within my body'

[hieroglyphs]

Xnm s-wDA atw, pr.n.k, r bw nfr Hn, i, im m sx(r)nS (srx), rn.i

unite/protect prosperous limbs, go-forth.of.you, to place happy speedily,
I, therein not make-stink, name.my

'the protector who made my limbs prosperous, go forth speedily to the happy place, do not make my name stink'

[hieroglyphs]

n Snywt, m Dd Grg, r.i, r gs nTr, nfrwy nfr sDm.k

to entourage, not say lies, to.me, to side god, how good, good hear.you

'to the entourage, do not speak lies against me near the god, how very good for you to hear'

Above the head of Anubis steadying the Balance

[hieroglyphs]

Dd mdw in, imi wt, im m, Hr pA, wTs mAat....(tx)....n mxAt

spoken words by, who-is-in place-embalming, therein behold, upon the, weigh
truth....plummet....of balance, according-to stand.its

'Words spoken by he who is in the place of embalming, therein behold the weighing of truthfulness and the plummet of the balance according to its stand'

Names of Two Goddesses standing left of the Balance

rnnt   msxnt

Renenet   Meskhenet

'Renenet, the Nurse Goddess and Meskhenet, the goddess of childbirth'

Beared Deity **Shay** wearing a tailed tunic and Standing Underneath and left of the Balance

SAy

Shay

'Shay, the god of Fate and Destiny'

Central right register of text over the balance, Anubis and Thoth

Dd mdw in, DHwty, wpt-mAa, n psDt, nTrw aA, nty m-bAH Awsir, sDm.tnw, mdt pn

spoken words by, Djhuty, judgement-truth, of Pesedjet, gods great, who-in presence Osiris, hear.they word this'

'Words spoken by Thoth, in judgement of Truth to the Great Ennead who are in the presence of Osiris, they hear this word'

m wn mAa, wTs of ib, n Awsir, iw bA.f, aHa m mtr, r.f

in real truth, weihed is/are ba-soul.his, stand as witness, to him

'as very truth, weighed of heart for Osiris, his ba-soul stands as a witness for him'

sp.f, mAa, Hr mxAt wr, nn gm, m ntw btA.f nb, nn xbi.f, Sbw

deeds.his, righteous, upon balance great, not found of/belonging-to wrong.him any, not diminish.he, food-offerings

'his deeds are righteous in the Great Balance and not any wrong has been found belonging to him, he did not diminish food offerings'

m rw-prw, nn HD.f, irytw, nn Sm.f, Xr rw.f

'in utterance-house, not harm/destroy.he, doings, not go.him, with mouth.his

'in the city temples, he did not do harm and he did not go about with his mouth'

nkAw Dr wn.n.f, tp tA

deceitful before/while exist.of.he, on earth

'deceitful while he was on earth.'

Top right register

Dd-mdw, psDt nTr aA, n DHwty, imi xmnw, Dd-mdw n st, nn prt, m rw.k

words-spoken, Ennead gods great, to Thoth, who-are-in Hermopolis, utterance of it, that-which comes-forth, from mouth.your

'Words spoken by the gods of the Great Ennead to Thoth, who is in Hermopolis, this utterance which comes forth from your mouth'

mAa, mt Awsir sS Anwy, mAa-xrw, nn btA, nn xsr.f, xr.nw

Truthful, straightforward/precise Osiris scribe Anwy, true-voice, no wrong/sin, no counsel-against.him, under.us

'is Truthful, straight-forward is Osiris Scribe, Anwy, True of Voice, there is no sin or accusation against him before us'

nn rdit sxm ammt im.f, rdi.tw, n.f, snw
not given power Ammit over.him, give.you, to.him food-offerings
'Ammit shall not be given power over him, let there be given to him food offerings'

prt m-bAh, Awsir, sAHt mn, m sxt Htpw, mi Smsw Hrw
come-forth in-presence-of Osiris, grant-of-land established, in field offerings, like followers Horus
'which come forth in the presence of Osiris and may a grant of land be established in the Field of Offerings, like the Followers of Horus'

PLATE IV: Horus Leads Anwy before Osiris, Isis and Nephthys

Dd mdw in, Hrw, sA st, ii.n xr.k, wn-nfr, ini.n n.k, Awsir Anwy
spoken words by, Horus, son Isis, come.of, to.you, Wen-nefer, bring.of, to.you, Osiris Anwy
'Words spoken by Horus, son of Isis, I have come to you Wen-nefer and I have brought to you Osiris Anwy'

ib.f, mAa, prt m mxAt, nn btA.f, xr nTr nb, nTrt nb

heart.his, true, come-forth from balance, no sinned.he, against god any, goddess any

**'his heart is true, he has come forth from the balance,
he has not sinned against any gods or any goddess'**

---

wDA n sw, DHwty, m sS, n psDt nTrw, r.f, mt mAat wr

judged of him, Thoth, in writing, spoken to Ennead, to.him, testify-concerning truth great

'Thoth has judged him (weighed his heart) in writing and told to the Ennead about him and testified concerning him the great truth'

---

imi rdi.tw, n.f, tAw Hnqt, prt m-bAH, Awsir, wn.n.f, mi Smsw, Hrw DtA

give/grant, give.you, to.him, bread beer, come-out in-presence, Osiris,
exist.of.he, like followers, Horus forever

**'may it be given to him bread and beer in the presence of Osiris,
may he be like the Followers of Horus, forever'**

Dd mdw in, Awsir A(nw)y, Dd.f, mk m-bAH.k, nb imntt

spoken words by, Osris Anwy, says.he, behold in-presence.your, lord west

'Words spoken by Osiris Anwy, 'Behold (I) am in your presence Lord of the West'

nn isft m Xt.i, nn Dd.n.i, grg m rx, nn sp-sn

not wrong-doing, in body.my, not said.of.i falsehood/lie, in/as know, not (misdeed) double

**'there is no wrongdoing in my body, I have not spoken lies knowingly,
and no double misdeed'**

imm wn.i, mi Hsy, nty imi-xt.k, Awsir Hsy aA, n nTr nfr

grant be.i, like favoured-ones, who member-bodyguard.your, Osiris favoured great, of god good

**'grant that I should be like the favoured ones who are members of your bodyguard,
Osiris greatly favoured of the good god'**

mrr, n nb tAwy, nsw sS, mAat, mry.f, Anwy, mAa-xrw, xr Awsir
loved, of lord two-lands, king scribe, true beloved.his, Anwy, true-voice, under Osiris
'beloved of the Lord of the Two-Lands, King's Scribe, Anwy, True of Voice under Osiris'

Text above Anwy's offering table as he kneels before Osiris

Awsir sS, Anwy
Osiris scribe, Anwy
'The Osiris Scribe, Anwy'

Text before Osiris and above the four sons of Horus standing upon a lotus flower

Awsir nb DtA	imsti	Hpy	dwA-mwt.f	qb-sn-w.f
Osiris lord eternity	Imseti	Happy	Duamutef	Qebsenuef
'Osiris Lord of Eternity, Imseti, Happy, Duamutef and Qebsenuef'				

The four sons of Horus: were a group of four gods in Egyptian religion, who were essentially the personifications of the four canopic jars, which accompanied mummified bodies.

Imseti	Duamutef	Hapy	Qebehsenuef
human form	**jackal** form	**baboon** form	**hawk** form
direction **South**	direction **East**	direction **North**	direction **West**
protected the **liver**	protected the **stomach**	protected the **lungs**	protected the **intestines**
protected by **Isis**	protected by **Neith.**	protected by **Nephthys**	protected by his mother **Serket**

PLATE 5: The Beginning of the Utterances of Coming Forth by Day
Top Register: shows the funeral procession of Anwy

HA m rw, nw prt, m hrw, sTsw sxAw

beginning of utterances, of coming-out, by day, praises recitations

'The beginning of utterances (Chapters) of coming forth by day, the praises and recitations'

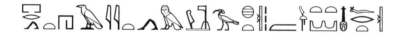

prt hAyt, m Xrt-nTr, Axwt m imntt, nfrt

coming-out going-in, under-god (necropolis), beneficial in west beautiful

'of coming forth and going into the Necropolis which is beneficial in the Beautiful West'

Ddt hrw, n qrs, aq m-xt, prt

spoken day, of burial, enter after, coming-out

'to be spoken on the day of burial going in and after coming out'

Dd mdw in, Awsir sS Anwy, inD-Hr.k, kA imntt

spoken words by, Osiris scribe Anwy, hail-to.you, bull west

'Words to be spoken by the Osiris Scribe Anwy, hail to you Bull of the West'

---

in DHwty, nswt HH, im.i, ink nTr aA, nm dpt

by/so-says Thoth, king eternity, therein.i, I god great of.in (who) boat

'so says Thoth, King of Eternity who therein I, I am the Great God in the Boat'

aHAy.n.i, Hr.k, ink wa, m nnw-n-nn, nTrw

fight.of.i, for.you, I one, of these-of-those, gods

'I have fought for you, I am one of these of those gods'

DA-DAt-t, s-maA-xrw, Awsir r xftyw.f, hrw pwy, n wDda words

magistrates-assessors, make-true-voice, Osiris against enemies.his, day that, of judgement words

'of the tribunal which made True of Voice (Vinicated) Osiris
against his enemies on that day of weighing of words'

n.wi, imytw.k, Awsir ink, m nnw, n nTrw, msw xrdw nwt

belong-of.I, in-the-midst-of.you, Osiris I, of these, of gods, fashioned children Nut

'I am in the midst of you, I am one of these gods who fashioned the children of Nut'

smAayw xtyw nw Awsir, xnri sbiw, Hr.f

slaughtered enemies for Osiris, captive/retrained rebels

'who slaughtered the enemies of Osiris and made captive the rebels'

---

n.wi, imitw.k, Hrw, aHA.n.i, Hr.k, sby.n.i, Hr rn.k

belong-of.i, in-company.your, Horus, fought.of.i, for.you, watched-over.of.i, over name.your

'I am in your company, O Horus, I have fought for you and watched over your name'

---

ink DHwty, s-mAa-xrw Awsir, r xtfyw.f, hrw pwy

I Thoth, make-true-voice Osiris, against enemies.his, day that

'I am Thoth, who made Osiris True of Voice against his enemies on that day'

𓄿 (hieroglyphs)
n wDA mdt, m Hwt-sr wr, imy iwnnw
of weighing words, in temple-official/prince great, who-is-in Heliopolis
'of weighing words in the Great Temple of the Prince, who is in Heliopolis'

(hieroglyphs)
ink Ddy, sA Ddy, iw im.i, Ddw, msy.i, m Ddw
I Djedy, conceived therein.i, Djedw, born.i, in Djedw
'I am Djedy (Busirite), conceived in Djedu (Busiris), I was born in Djedu (Busiris)'

(hieroglyphs)
wn.i, Hna HAi, iAkbyt, Awsir m tAwy-rextt
am.i, together-with men-weepers, women-mourners, Osiris in/from ends-of-earth
'I am together with the men weepers and women who mourned Osiris from the Ends of the Earth'

s-mAa-xrw Awsir, r xftyw.f, xrw.stw, ra DHwty, s-mAa-xrw Awsir, r xftyw.f

made-true-voice (victorious) Osiris, against enemies.his, say.they, Ra and Thoth, made-true-voice Osiris, against enemies.his

'and who made Osiris victorious against his enemies, the words they say, Ra and Thoth has made Osiris victorious against his enemies'

---

xrw.tw, n.i, DHwty wn.i, Hna Hrw, hrw Hbs, tS-tS

say.one, for.i, Thoth am.i, together-with Horus day clothing crushed/dismembered-one

'said for me, Thoth, that I am with Horus on the day of clothing the dismembered one'

---

wn t(T)p-htw, n iaw, wrd ib

opening pit-of snake/cavern, for washing, weary heart-one

'and opening the caverns for washing the one of weary heart (Inert One)'

𓏛𓏤 𓈖 𓊃𓌕𓏏 (𓋴𓊠𓏏) 𓅓 𓂋𓏤𓋴𓍿𓂝𓏤𓏌

sS rw, n sSyt (sStA), m rw-sTA-w

open mouth/door, of secrets, in Ru-setja-u

'and opening the door of secrets in Rosetjau (Necropolis)'

𓃹𓈖𓏤𓀀𓏤𓅆𓂋𓄿𓏤𓂝𓏤𓊃𓊪𓅆𓇋𓌻𓏭𓈖𓊨𓅆𓇋𓐝𓊃𓐍𓅓

wn.i, Hna Hrw, m nD, qaH pwy, iAby n Awsir, imy sxm

am.i, with Horus, as protector, arm that, left of Osiris, who-is-in Sekhem (shrine/temple town)

'I am with Horus as protector of that left arm of Osiris who is in Sekhem (Letopolis)'

𓅡𓏤𓂻𓂋𓏤𓂻𓅓𓇋𓅓𓅓𓏌𓏤𓇳𓏤𓂧𓂋𓋴𓃀𓏤𓀀𓅆𓅓𓊃𓐍𓅓⊗

aq.i, prw.i, m immw, hrw dr, sbiw m sxm

enter.i, come-out.i, among those-who-are-in day destroying, rebels in Sekhem

'I go in and I come out among those who are in the day of destroying the rebels in Sekhem'

𓃭𓋴𓏤𓄿𓃀𓊪𓁷𓂋𓅱𓉐𓁹𓏏𓊨𓊪𓇌𓂻𓏏𓅆𓏤𓏥

wn.i, Hna Hrw, hrw Hbw, nw Awsir, ir aAbt

exist/am.i, with Horus, day festivals, of Osiris, do offerings

'I am with Horus on the day of the festivals of Osiris, making offerings'

(hieroglyphs)

hrw 6, nt Hb dnit, m iwnw, ink wab, m Ddw

day 6, of festival Denit in Heliopolis, I wab-priest, in Djedu (Busiris)

'on day six of the festival of Denit in Heliopolis, I am the wab-priest in Busiris'

(hieroglyphs)

rw, imi pr Awsir, sqAy tA, ink mAA

lion-god, who-is-in house Osiris, raise-up (gods) land, I see

'to the Lion God who is in the House of Osiris, with the gods who raise up the earth, I see'

StAw, m r-sTAw pn, ink Sd Hbt, n bA, m Ddw

secrets, in Rosetju this, I read festival/ritual-book, for ba-soul, in Djedu

'the secrets in this Rosetju, I read the Book of Ritual for the Ba-Soul in Busiris'

---

ink sm, m iryw.f, ink wr xrp-Hrt, hrw rdit

I sem-priest, with duties.his, I great controller-craftsmen, day placing

**'I am the Sem-Priest with his duties,
I am the Great Controller of the Craftsmen on the day of placing'**

Hnw-skr, Hr maxAyt.tw.f

Henu-Bark-Sokar, upon sledge.one.its

'the Henu-Bark of Sokar upon its sledge'

[hieroglyphs]
ink sSp xbAsy, hrw xbs tA, m nni-nswt
I take-up hoe, day ploughing land, in Child-Royal-City
'I take up the hoe on the day of ploughing the land in the City of the Royal Child (Heracleopolis)'

PLATE 6: Procession of mourners, the Sem-Priest, Mummy of Anwy and his wife Tutu

[hieroglyphs]
i s-tknyw bA mnx, m pr Awsir, s-tkn.nw, bA iqr, n Awsir
O! make-draw-near, soul well-established, in house Osiris, make-draw-near.you, soul excellent of Osiris
'O you, who cause to draw near the well established soul in the house of Osiris, you cause to draw near the excellent soul of Osiris'

[hieroglyphs]
sS Anwy mAa-xrw, Hna.tnw, r pr Awsir, sDm.f.tn, mAA.f
scribe Anwy true-voice, with.you. to house Osiris, hear,he.you, see.he
'Scribe Anwy, True of Voice, together with you, to the House of Osiris, may he hear you, may he see'

mi mAA.tnw, aHa.f, mi aHa.tnw, Hmsi.f, mi Hmsi.tnw
like see.you, stand.he, like stand.you, sit.he, like sit.you
'like you, see, may he stand, like you, stand, may he sit, like you, sit'

i ddyw, tAw Hnqt, n bAw mnxw, m pr, Awsir
O! give-doubly, bread beer, for souls perfected, in house, Osiris
'O you who gave bread and beer for the perfected souls in the house of Osiris'

rdi.tnw, tAw Hnqt, r trwy, n bA, n Awsir Anwy, mAa-xrw
give.you, bread beer, to/at season-dual, for soul, of Oisiris Anwy, true-voice
'You give bread and beer at the seasons for the ba-soul of Osiris Anwy, True of Voice'

xr nTrw nbw, tA-wr mAa-xrw, Hna.tnw, i wnyw wat, wpwy matennw

under gods all, Abydos-Nome true-voice, with.you, hail openers way, openers roads

**'under all the gods of Abydos (Thinite) Nome, hail to you,
openers of the way, openers of the roads'**

n bAw mnxw, m pr, n Awsir, wn irf.tnw, n.f, wat

for ba-souls perfected in house of Osiris, open now.you, to.him way

'for the ba-souls perfected in the house of Osiris, open you now for him the way'

wpw irf.tnw, matnnw, n bA, n Awsir sS

open now.you, roads, for soul, of Osiris scribe

'open you now the roads for the ba-soul of Osiris the scribe'

Hsb Htp, nTrw nbw, Anwy, Hna.tnw, aq.f, m dnd
reckon offerings, gods all, Anwy, with.you, enter.he, with confidence
'reckoner of offerings of all the gods, Anwy, with you may he enter freely with confidence'

pr.f, m Htp, m pr Awsir, nn xsf.tw.f, nn Sna.tw.f
come-out.he, with peace, from house Osiris, not repelled.one.he, not turned-back.one.he
'and may he come out with peace from the house of Osiris, may one not repel him or turn him back'

aq.f, Hsw, prw.f, mrw, mAa-xrw.f
enter.he, beloved, come-out.he, true-voice.he
'May he go in favoured, may he come out loved, may he be victorious'

ir wddwt.f, m pr Awsir, Sm.f, mdwt.f, Hna.tnw

done commands.he, in house Osiris, go.he, speech.he, with.you

'may his commands be done in the House of Osiris, may he go and speak with you'

Ax.f, Hna.tnw, nn gmn.tw, wn.f, im

akh-spirit.he, with.you, not find.one, fault.him, therein

'may he be an akh-spirit with you, may you not find fault in him'

---

iw, maxAt, sSw.ti, m sp.f

behold, balance empty.it, misdeeds.his

'behold, the balance is empty of his misdeeds'

r n rdit, r(A) n Awsir sS, Hsb Htp, nTrw nbw, Anwy, mAa-xrw, n.f, m Xrt-nTr

utterance giving, mouth to Osiris scribe, reckoner offerings, gods all, Anwy, true-voice, to.him, in necropolis (Under-God)

'Utterance for giving a mouth to the Osiris Scribe, reckoner of offerings of all the gods, Anwy, True of Voice (Victorious) in the God's Necropolis (Underworld)'

Dd-mdw, iw.i, wbn kwi, m swHt, imit tA StA

spoken-words, behold.i, arise.i, from egg, which-in land secret

'Words to be spoken: 'Behold I, I have arisen from the egg which is in the secret land'

iw, rdiw n.i, r(A).i, mdw.i, im.f, m-bAH, nTr aA

behold/is/are, given to.me, mouth.my, speak.i, with.it, before, god great

'behold my mouth given to me that I may speak with it before the Great God'

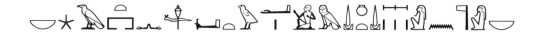

nb dwA, nn xsf.tw, a.i, m DADAt n nTr nb

lord dwat, not drive-away.one, hand.my, in tribunal god any

'Lord of the Duat, do not drive away my hand in the tribunal of any god'

ink Awsir, nb r(A)-sTAw, psS Awsir, Anwy, mAa-xrw

I Osiris, lord Rostejau, share Osiris scribe, Anwy, true-voice

'I am Osiris Lord of Rosetjau, who shares with the Osiris Scribe, Anwy, True of Voice'

m nnw nty, tp.f, xt, ii.n.i, r mrr ib.i, m iw-nsrsr

with that who, on.it, dais, come.of.i, to wish heart.my, in lake-fire (Iw-Neserser)

'with that who is on the Dais, I have come for what my heart desires in the Lake of Fire'

axm.n.i, inD.k, nb sSp, xnty Hwt, Hry-tp

quench.of.i, hail-to.you, lord bright-light, foremost temple chief

'I have quenched, hail to you, Lord of the Bright Light, foremost of the Chief Temple'

kkw smAw, ii.n.i, xr.k, Axw wab kwi

darkness twilight, come.of.i, under.you, glorious-spirit pure I

'in darkness and twilight, I have come, a glorious spirit and I am pure'

awy.i, HA-tp.k, dniw.k, tpw-aw.k

hands-dual.my, behind.you, portion.your, ancestors.your

'my hands are about you, your portion, (is with) your ancestors'

ﾋ ﾛ ｸ ｲ ﾒ ﾑ (hieroglyphs)
rdi.k, n.i, r(A).i, mdw.i, im.f, sSm.i, ib
give.you, to.me, speech.i, with.it, guide.me, heart
'give you to me, my mouth, that I may speak with it, guide my heart'

(hieroglyphs)
n wnwt.f, nbdt grH
at hour.it, fire night
'at its hour of fire and night'

A promise on the freedom of the soul of the deceased

ir rx mDAt tn, tp tA, m sSw, Hr qrs, r.i, pw
if know book this, on land, in writing, upon coffin, utterance.my, this
'this book is known on land or in writing upon a coffin, this utterance of mine'

iw.f, pr.f, m hrw, m xprw nb, mr.f, hna aq r st

behold.he, come-out.he, with forms any, desires.he, and enter to place

'behold he shall come out with any form he desires and enter his place'

nn Snarw.tw.f, iw rdi.tw, n.f, tAw Hnqt, wr n iwf

not turn-back.on.you, behold give.one, to him, bread beer, great of flesh/meat

'without being turned back, behold one given to him bread and beer and best of meat'

Hr xAyt nt Awsir, iw.f, aq.he, m Htp, r sxt-iArw

upon table-offerings of Osiris, is.he, in peace, enter.he, to field-reeds

'upon the table of offerings of Osiris, he shall enter in peace to the Field of Reeds'

[hieroglyphs]
r rx, wDw pn, n imt Ddw, iw rdi.tw, n.f, ity bdt, im.s
to know, command this, of who-in Djedu, is give.one, to.him, barley emmer, in.it
'to know this command of who are in Busiris to him is given, barley and emmer therein it'

[hieroglyphs]
wnn xr.f, wAD mi, wn n.f, tp tA, iw.f, ir.f, mrt.f
be with.him, health like, exist/was of.he, upon earth, is.he, do.he, desires.he
'there shall be with him strong health like he was upon the earth, he shall do as he desires'

[hieroglyphs]
n mi, nn nTrw-9, nty m dwAt, m Ss mAa
of like, those gods-9, who-are in Duat, in bond truth
'like those Nine Gods who are in the Duat (Underworld) in bonds of Truth'

𓀋 𓏥 𓈖 𓊗 𓇋𓅱 𓁹 𓋴𓈙 𓆊 𓏭𓏤 𓏪
HHw n sp, iw, Awsir sS Anwy
millions of times, behold, Osiris scribe Anwy
'a million times, behold, the Osiris Scribe, Anwy'

PLATE 7: Utterance 17

Anwy and and his wife Tutu sat in a booth playing senet before their Ba-bird soul forms which are sat upon a shrine. Around the central Akhet (horizon)-Sky sign sits the two lions of Tomorrow and Yesterday, the Bennu Bird stands before the bier of Anwy's mummy, where each side sits two falcons with the headress signs of Isis and Nepthys

HAt m s-wTs, sxw prt, hAyt m Xrt-nTr, Axwt m imntt nfrt

beginning of praises, recitations coming-out, going-in of Kheret-Netjer, glorious in west beautiful

'The beginning of praises and recitations of coming out and going in of the Necropolis, glorious in the West'

prt m hrw, m xprw nb, mry.f, Hba

coming-out by day, in forms all, desire.he, playing at snt

'coming out by day in all forms he desires, playing at Senet'

[hieroglyphs]

Hmsi sH, prt m bA anxy

sit booth, coming-out as ba-soul living

'sitting in a booth, coming out as a living soul'

[hieroglyphs]

Dd mdw in, Awsir sS Anwy, m-xt mni.f, iw Axwt

spoken words by, Osiris scribe Anwy, after die.he, is/are glorious

'Words spoken by the Osiris Scribe Anwy, after he has died, it is glorious

---

[hieroglyphs]

n ir.s, tp tA, xpr mdwt nbt, tm inwk, tm m-wn

to do.it on earth, become words all, Atum, I Atum in-existing

'to do it on earth, bring into being all words, I am Atum, Atum when'

𓏤𓄿𓇋𓆣𓏤𓀁𓆓𓈖𓏌𓏌𓏌𓈖𓀀𓏤𓇳𓀀𓅱𓂋𓄣𓇳𓇋𓅆𓏤𓇳𓅆
wa kwi, xpr.n.i, m nw, ink ra, m xay.f, m SAa
one I, become.of.i, in Nu, I Ra, in rising, in beginning
'I was one alone, I came into being in the Primordial Waters of Nu, I am Ra in glorious appearance in the beginning'

𓊪𓂝𓅓𓈖𓈖𓆑𓊪𓅱𓉔𓂋𓀁𓄿𓅓𓇋𓅆𓅆𓇳𓅆
HqA pn, n.f, pw tri, rf sw pw, m SAa
ruler this, of.him, who, forsooth/pray, then/now him, Ra this/who, in beginning
'who is this ruler of him? pray then is Ra who was in the beginning'

𓆄𓅆𓈖𓈖𓇋𓈖𓋴𓅱𓈖𓋴𓅱𓏏𓏠𓈖𓏏𓆣𓋴𓍿𓋴𓆄𓅱
xaa.f, m nni-nsw, m nswt, m wnt, nn xpr, sTs Sw
appearance.his, in Heracleopolis, as king, in reality, not become pillars-Shu
'when his appearance in Heracleopolis (Nini-Nesu) as king before the Pillars of Shu existed'

(hieroglyphs)
iw.f, Hr AqAq, n imy xmnw, ink nTr aA
is.he, upon hill, of which-is-in Hermopolis, I god great
'he was upon the <u>hill</u> of that which is in Hermopolis (Khenemu: Eight-Town), I am the great god'

(hieroglyphs)
xpr Dsf, nw pw, qmA rn.f, psDt nTrw, m nTr
come-into-being himself, Nu (god) that-is, created name.his, Pesedjet gods, as god
'who came into being of himself, this god Nu, who created his name, as god, of the Ennead of gods'

(hieroglyphs)
pw tri rf sw, pw Ra, qmA rn, n at.f
who? pray then him, Ra it-is, created name, of members.his
'pray, who then is he? it is Ra, who created the names of his members'

xpr nn pw, m nTrw, imy-xt, Ra, ink nty, xsf.f, m nTrw

come-into-existence these it-is, as gods, who-are-in-attendance,
Ra, I-am not, opposed.he, among gods

'having come into existence of those it is as gods, who are in attendance of Ra,
I am he who is not opposed among the gods'

pw tri rf sw, tm pw, imy itn,f, ky Dd

who? pray then him, Temw it-is, who-is-in Aten-disk.his, another say

'pray, who then is he? it is Atum, who is in his sun-disk (Aten), otherwise said:'

ra pw, m wbn.f, m Axt iAbty, nt pt, ink sf

Ra it-is, in rising.he, in horizon eastern, of heaven, I-am yesterday

'Ra it is, in his rising in the eastern horizon, I am yesterday.'

rx wi, dwAw, pw tri rf sw

know I, tomorrow, who pray then him?

'I know tomorrow, who then pray is he?'

---

ir sf, Asir pw, ir dwAw, ra pw, hrw pwy n

as-to yesterday, Osiris it-is, as-to tomorrow, Ra that, day of

'as to yesterday it is Osiris, as to tomorrow, that is Ra on the day of'

---

sHtm xftyw.f, nw nbr-Dr, im.f, Hna s-HqA.tw

destroy enemies.his, of Neber-Djer, in.it, with made-ruler.you

**'destroying his enemies in it of Neber-Djer (Lord to End),
together with the ruler you appointed'**

sA.f, Hrw, ky Dd, hrw pwy, n iw.nw-mn-Hb, dhn ntw qrs

son.his, Horus, day that, of are.we-established-festival, to-appoint burial

'his son, Horus, on that day of 'We-are-Established-Festival,' to appoint the burial'

pw nt Awsir, in it ra, ir.n.tw, aHA nTrw, xft wDw.nw

this-it-is of Osiris, by father Ra, made.of.one, fighting gods, when commanded.us

'this it is of Osiris by his father Ra, to make the battle of the gods when commanded us'

Awsir, r nb imntt, pw tri rf sw, imntt pw, ir.n.tw, r bAw nTrw

Osiris, to lord west, what pray then it?, west it-is, made.of.one, for souls gods

'Osiris as Lord of the Western Desert, what then pray is it?
it is the Western Desert made for the souls of the gods'

xft wDw Awsir, r spAt imntt, ky Dd, imntt pw, nnw pw, rdi n ra

when commanded Osiris, to nome west, another-way saying, west this-it-is, that, made of Ra

'when Osiris commanded to the Wertern Desert Nome, another way of saying: the Western Desert, this it is, that Ra made'

---

hAy nTr nb.s, aHa aHA.n.f, Hr.s

go-down god any, stand fight.of.he, upon.it

'descend any god, he stands and fights for it'

---

iw.i, rx.kwi, nTr pwy, nty im.s, pw ptri rf sw

behold.i, know.i, god that in.it, who pray then he

'behold I know that god who is in it, pray, who then is he?'

[hieroglyphs]
Awsir pw, ky Dd, ra rn.f, Hnnw pw, n ra
Osiris it-is, another saying. Ra name.his, phallus it-is, of Ra
'it is Osiris, another way of saying, his name is Ra, it is the phallus of Ra'

[hieroglyphs]
nk.f, im.f, Dsf, ink bnnw pwy, nty im iwnnw
copulate.him, with.he, himself, I-am Bennu-Bird, that which-is-in Heliopolis
'when he copulated with himself, I am that Bennu Bird which is in Heliopolis'

[hieroglyphs]
ink iry-sipw, n nty wnn, pw tri rf sw
I-am, inspector, of that-which-is exists, who pray then he
'I am the inspector of that which exists, pray, who then is he?'

Awsir pw, ky Dd, XAt.f, pw, ky Dd, n r nHH, pw

Osiris it-is, another say, corpse.his, it-is, another say, for to eternity, it-is

'it is Osris, another way of saying, it is his corpse, another saying, for to eternity it is'

hrw ir, DtA pw, grH pw, ink mnw, m prw.f

day as-to, eternity it-is, night it-is, I-am Min, in going-forth.his

'the day, as to eternity, night it is, I am Min in his going forth'

iw rdi n.i, Swty.f, m tp.i, pw tri rf sw, mnw Hrw, pw

behold/is/are, given to.me, two-plumes.his, on head.my, what-it-is pray then it, Min Horus it-is

'behold may his Two-Plumes be given to me on my head.
pray what then is it? Min, it is Horus'

nD Hr it.f, ir prw n.f, msw.f, pw ir Swty.f, m tp.f

protector over father.his, as-for going-forth, it-is birth.his, it-is two-plumes.his, on head.his

'protector of his father, as for going forth, it is his birth, it is his Two Plumes on his head'

Smt st Hna nb-Hwt, rdi.n.snw, sw, Hr tp.f

going Isis with Nephthys, placed.of.they. it upon head.his

'are the going of Isis and Nephthys and placing themselves upon his head'

---

wn.n.snw, m Drttwy, sikA.snw, Hr mn, tp.f, ky Dd

exist.they as kites-dual, promote/adorn.they, upon lacking, head.his, another say

'they exist as the Two-Kites adorning a space upon his head, another saying:'

arwt wrt aAt, pw, imyt tp it.snw
uraeus-dual great very, it-is, in-head father.their
'the Great and Mighty Two Uraei it is, which are on the head of their father'

PLATE 8: Chapter 17 (continued)

Upper register left: The blue skinned god of eternity, Heh, kneels holding the notched palm branch of millions of years with his right hand while his left hand hovers over a snake cartouche, the Lake of Natron. A diety, River-is-his-Name, stands with arms outstretched; his right hand is over the Wadj-wer (Great Green Sea, the Mediteranean) and his left hand is over the Lake of Maat. Centre left are two shrines with doors and the Left Eye of Horus. Right side of the upper register sits Meh-Weret (Great Flood Waters), the horned Celestial Cow Goddess with sun disk, a form of Hathor and mother of Ra. Either side of 'The Mound of Abydos' stands the sons of Horus, Hapy, Imsety and Duamutef and Qebehsenuef, which represent the four cardinal points, North, South, and East, West respectively. A deity emerges from the sacred mound holding two ankh signs, the signs of Life.

Top Register Text - Left to Right

HHw
Hehw god
'Hehw, the god of eternity, god of millions of years'

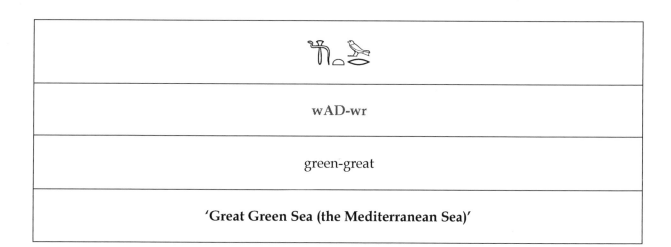

wAD-wr

green-great

'Great Green Sea (the Mediterranean Sea)'

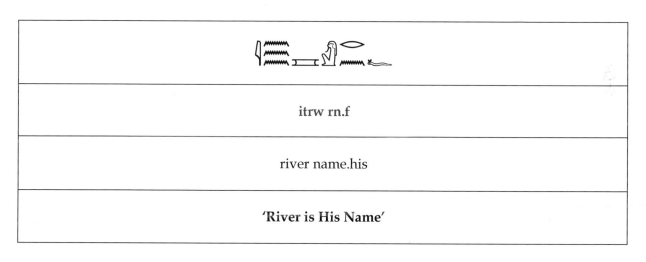

itrw rn.f

river name.his

'River is His Name'

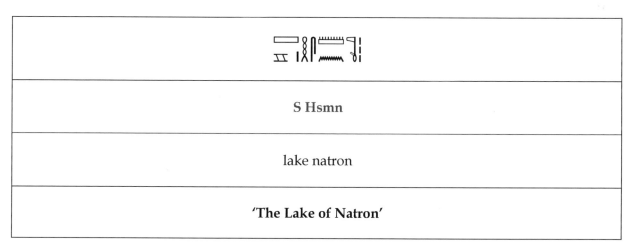

S Hsmn

lake natron

'The Lake of Natron'

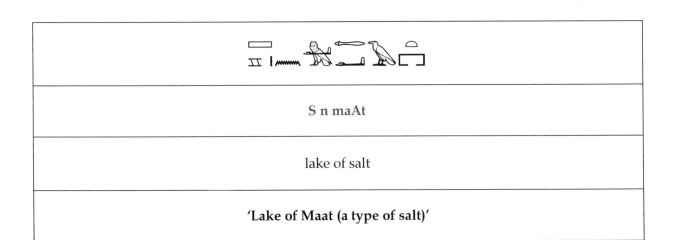

S n maAt

lake of salt

'Lake of Maat (a type of salt)'

---

r-sTAw pwy

necropolis that

'That Necropolis (Rosetjau)'

mH-wrt, HsAt, irt ra

flood-waters-great (Meh-Weret, sacred sky cow, a form of Hathor and wife of Ra), eye Ra

'The Great Flood Waters (Meh-Weret, Celestial Cow Goddess), the Eye of Ra'

imsti	Hpy	dwAmwt.f	qbsnw.f

Imsety Hapy Duamutef Qebsenuef

'The Four Sons of Horus'

iAt AbDw

mound Abydos

'The Mound of Abydos'

Bottom Register Text

tm, ky Dd, n irwy.f, pw Swty.f, m tp.f, wnn Awsir sS, Htp nTrw nbw, Anwy

Atum, another say, of eyes-dual.his, it-is plumes-dual.his, on head.his,
exist Osiris scribe, gods all, Anwy

'Atum, said another way, for his Two Eyes are his Two Plumes on his head, exists Osiris Scribe, offering of the all the gods, Anwy'

im mAa-xrw, m tA.f, ii.n.f, m niwt.f, pw tri rf sw

in true-voice, in land.his, come.of.him, in city.his, what pray then it?

'in victory in his land, he comes into his city, pray, what then is it?'

Axt pw, nt it.f, tmw, dr.i, iwtw.i

horizon it-is, of father.his, Atum, destroy.i, wrongdoing.my

'it is the horizon of his father Atum, I destroy my wrongdoing'

xsr.i, Dwt.i, pw itr rf sw

drive-away.i, evil, what pray then it

'I drove away evil, pray then what is it?'

Sad.tw, XpAw pw, n Awsir sS Anwy, mAa-xrw, xr nTrw nbw

cut-off.one, navel-chord it-is, of Osiris Scribe Anwy, true-voice, under gods all

'it is that the navel chord cut off of Osiris Scribe Anwy, True of Voice, under all the gods'

---

sHr.tw, Dwt nb, iry.f, pw itr rf sw

removed.one, evil all, belonging-to.him, what pray then it?

'all the evil has been removed from him, pray, what then is it?'

---

wab pw, m hrw, n mswt.f, wabw.i, m sSwy.i

purification it-is, in day, of birth.my, purified.i, in nests/marshes-dual.my

'it is the purification on the day of my birth, I am prified in my Two Nests'

𓉐𓏏𓄿𓀀𓈖𓈖𓏌𓇓𓏏𓉐𓏤𓇳𓅃𓏤𓏏𓃂𓃀𓏏𓀀𓁐
aAt nty, m nni-nsw, hrw pwy, n aAbt rxit
great very, which in child-royal-city, day that, of offerings people
' very great, which is in Neni-Nsw (City of the Royal Child), on that day of offerings of the people'

𓈖𓀭𓅃𓏥𓂋𓈖𓅃𓏏𓉐𓇓𓀀𓂋𓆑𓅪
n nTr pwy, aA nty, im.s, pw itr rf sw
to god that, great who, in.it, what pray then it?
'to the great god who is in it, pray, what then is it?'

𓁍𓏤𓏤𓀀𓏏𓆛𓅃𓏤𓏤𓏏𓀀𓈖𓉐𓅃𓈖𓈔𓌪
HHw, rn n wa, wAD-wr, rn n ky, S pw, n Hsmn
Heh, name of one, Green-Great, name of another, lake it-is, of natron
'Hehw (God of Eternity) is the name of one, the Great Green Sea is the name of the other, Lake it is of Natron'

Hna S pw, n maAt, ky Dd, sSmw HHw, rn n wa

with lake, of salt, another say, guide/lead Hehw, name of one

'with Lake of Salt, another saying: Leader of Millions of Years, is the name of one'

---

waD-wri, rn n ky, ky Dd, wtt HHw, rn n wa

green-great, name of another, another say, begetter Hehw, name of one

'the Great Green Sea is the name of another, another saying:
Begetter of Hehw is the name of one'

---

wAD-wri, rn n ky, ir Xrt, nTr aA, nty im.s, ra pw Dsf

green-great, name of another, as-to concerning, god great, who in.it, Ra it-is self.him

'the Great Green Sea is the name of another, as to concerning the Great God,
who is in it, Ra it is himself'

(hieroglyphs)	
Sm.n.i, Hr wat, rx.n.i, tpw m iw-mAat, pw tri rf sw	
go/pass.of.i, upon way, know.of.i, heads of island-truth, what pray then it	
'I passed upon the way I know in front of the Island of Truth, pray what then is it?'	

(hieroglyphs)	
ir r-sTAw pw, sbAwt pw rsyt, nAirw.f	
as-to Rosetjau it-is, door southern it-is Nairw-ef	
'as to Rosetjau it is the southern door, it is Nairw-ef'	

(hieroglyphs)	
sbAwt mHty, n iAt, ir Xrt, iw-mAat, AbDw pw	
door northern, of mound, as-to concerning island-maat, Abydos it-is	
'the northern door of the Mound, as concerning the Island of Truth, it is Abydos'	

(hieroglyphs)
ky Dd, wat pw, Smt n it.f, tm Hr.s, xft wDA.f
another say, road it-is, go of father.his, Temu upon.it, when set-out.he
'Another saying: it is the road went of my father Temu, when he proceeded'

(hieroglyphs)
r sxt iArw, pw, mst DfAwy, n nTrw
to field reeds, it-is, bring-forth provisions, for gods
'to the Field of Reeds which brings forth provisions for the gods'

(hieroglyphs)
HA-tp kAri, ir-Xrt, sbAt pw, Dsrt sbAt pw
around shrine, as-to-concerning, door it-is, sacred, door it-is
'who are around the shrine, as to concerning the sacred door, the door it is'

n sTs Sw-pt, ir sbA mHty, dwAt pw

of pillars-of-heaven Shu, as-to door northern, of/for duat it is

'of Shu's Pillars of Heaven, as to the northern door, it is for the Duat'

---

ky Dd, aAwy-rAwy, pwy wDA, n Temu, Hr.f

another saying: door-dual-gate, that goes, of Temu, through.it

'another way said, the Double Door Gates that Temu goes through'

Axt iAbty, nt pt, imyw-bAH, ima n.i, awy.tnw

horizon eastern, of heaven, those-who-are-in-presence.my, give to.me, two-arms.your

'in the Eastern Horizon of Heaven, those who are in my presence, give to me your hands'

ink nTr pwy, n xpr.n.i, imi.tnw, pw tri rf sw

I god that, of become.of.i, aming.you, what pray then it?

'I am the god who has come into existence among you, pray, what then is it?'

snfw pw, pr m Hnnw, ra m-xt, wA.f, r irt

blood it-is, come-forth from phallas, Ra after, way.his, to do

'it is blood from the phallus of Ra after he went to act'

Sad im.f-Dsf, aHa.nw, xpr m nTrw, imyw-xt ra

cut-off therein.him himself, arise.we, came-into-being among gods, those-following-after Ra

'to cut himself, we arose and came into being, those following after Ra'

Hw Hna saa, wn.n.snw, m-xt tmu
god-Hu with god-Saa, exist.of.they, following-after Temu
'the (primeval creator) gods, they came into being following after Temu'

Saa, god, Sia or Saa, a primeval god seen in the solar bark at the creation, he also had a connection with writing and was often shown holding a papyrus scroll. This papyrus was thought to embody intellectual achievements. It was said that Atum created the two gods Saa and Hu from his blood spilled while cutting his own penis, a possible reference to circumcision.

Sia appeared standing on the Solar barge during its journey through the night in New Kingdom underworld texts and tomb decorations, together with Hu, 'creative utterance' and Heka (god) the god of magic. These gods were seen as special powers helping the creator.

Hu, god, Hu (ḥw), in ancient Egypt, was the deification of the first word, the word of creation, that Atum was said to have exclaimed upon ejaculating or, alternatively, his self-castration, in his masturbatory act of creating the Ennead, by the time of Ptolemaic Egypt, Hu had merged with Shu (air).

ma Xrt, hrw nt hrw, nb, iw mH.n.i, Awsir sS Anwy, mAa-xrw
behold duty day of day, every, filled/restored.of.i, Osiris scribe Anwy, true-voice
'in the duty day of every day, I restored, Osiris Scribe Anwy, True of Voice,'

n.k, wDAt, m-xt hAb-mr.s, hrw n aHA

for.you, Wedat, following-after, sent-injured.it, day of fight

'for you the Eye of Horus following after it was injured on the day of fighting'

---

rHwy, pw tri rf sw, hrw pwy, n aHA

combatants-dual, what pray then it? day it-is, of fight

'of the Two Combatants (Horus and Seth), what then pray is it? the day of fighting'

Hrw im.f, Hna stX, m wd sTA, m Hr Hrw

Horus in.it, with Setekh (Seth), from inflict injury, in face Horus

'of Horus in it with Seth (Setekh) with inflicting injury in the face of Horus'

[hieroglyphs]
iTi Hrw Xrwy, n stX, in Xrt DHwty, ir nn
took Horus under-dual, of Seth, by under/possessing Thoth, did this
'when Horus took away Seth's testicles, it was Horus who did this'

[hieroglyphs]
m Dba.fy, Ds.f, m sTs.n.i, Snw m tri, n nSny
with fingers, self.him, in raise-up.of.i, hair in time, of rage
'with his finger himself, I lifted up the hair at the time of rage'

[hieroglyphs]
pw tri rf sw, irt pw, imnt n ra, m nSny, r.f, m-xt
what pray then it? eye it-is, right of Ra, in rage, against.him, following-after
'what pray then is it? it is the Right Eye of Ra when it raged against him, following after'

hAby.f sw, in DHwty, Ts Sny im
send.he it, by Dhjwty, raise-up hair therein
'he had sent it, by Djhwty (Thoth) who lifted up the hair therein'

ini.n.f, n anx wDA snb, nn bgA (bgAi?) n nb, ky Dd, wnn irt pw, m mr.s, m
brought.of.he, to life prosperity health, not harm of any, another saying, exist eye this, as sick, when
'when he brought it to Life, Prosperity and Health, without harm any harm, another saying, this Eye was sick, when'

PLATE 9: Top register displays eleven named and seated gods: Continuing Utterance 17
The Eleven Deities from Left to Right

mAA-it.f   Xry-bAq.f   Hrw-xnty-irty   inpw
see.father.his, under-moringa-tree.his, Horus-foremost-eyes, Anubis
'Maa-it-ef (he who sees his father), Khery-baq-ef (he who is under the moringa tree), Horus-khenty-irety (Horus Foremost of Two Eyes), Inpw (Anubis)'

𓂜𓇥𓎛𓂜𓇥𓎛 𓅡𓃀𓈎𓂧𓂧 𓈋𓈖𓏏𓎛𓎛𓆑
nDH-nDH, iA-qd-qd, xnty-hh.f
Nedjeh-Nedjeh, Ia-qed-qed, Khenty-heh.ef
' the deities, Nedjeh-Nedjeh, Ia-qed-qed, Khenty-heh.ef (one who is in front of his brazier)'

imy-wnt.f, dSr-mAA, stHn, mAA-im-grH, ini-im-hrw
Imy-wenut.ef, Deshr-maa, Sethen, Maa-im-gereh, Ini-im-heru
'Imy-wenut.ef (He who is in his hour), Deshr-maa (Red Eyes), Sethen (Radiant One), Maa-im-gereh (who sees in the Night), Ini-im-heru (who brings the Day)'

𓈖𓈖𓏤𓏛 𓁷𓂋𓅓𓇋 𓈖 𓏏𓈖𓅱𓆑 𓊢𓂝 𓇋𓂋𓆑 𓅭𓏏𓏭 𓂋 𓊪𓋴𓎼 𓈖𓋴
wnn.s, Hr rmy, n snw.f, aHa irf DHwty, r psAg (psg), n.s
exist.it, upon weeping, for second-time.it, stand then Thoth to spit, to it
'it was weeping for a second time, then Thoth stands to spit on it'

iw, mAA.n.f, ra, ms m sf, r xpdwt, n mH-wrt

behold, seen.of.i, Ra, born of yesterday, of buttocks, of Meh(flood-waters)-Weret (great)

'Behold I have seen Ra, born of yesterday, from the rear end of Meh-Weret (Great Flood Waters), the Celestial Cow goddess'

Meh-Weret: was the goddess of flooding water, a goddess related to creation and to rebirth. Her name means 'Great Flood', linking her with water and the primeval waters of Nun. In the Old Kingdom, she was believed to have helped the pharaoh and Ra reach the sky, by way of the Nile in the underworld.

wDA.f, wDA.i, Ts-pXr, pw tri rf sw

prosperity.his, prosperity.my, vice-versa (phrase/sentence-turn/go-around), what pray then it?

'His prosperity, my prosperity, and vice versa, pray then, what is it?'

nnw nnwi, n pt, ky Dd, twt pw, n irt ra, dwAw.tw

these-of waters, of heaven, another saying, image it-is, of eye RA, morning.it

**'These are waters (Nenui) of heaven, another saying,
it is the image of the Eye of Ra, on the morning'**

r msw.tw.f, hrw nb, ir mH-wrt, wDAt pw, n Ra

at birth.one.its, day every, as-to Great-Flood-godess, Wedjat-Eye it-is, of Ra

**'at its birth every day, as to the Great Flood Goddess, the Celestial Cow,
Meh-Weret, it is the Wedat Eye of Ra'**

Hr-nty, ir Awsir sS Anwy, mAa-xrw, wa wr, m nnw nTrw, imyw

because that/which/who, as-to Osiris Scribe Anwy, true-voice,
one great, as those gods, who-are-in

'because that as Osiris Scribe Anwy, True of Voice, the great one, as those gods who are in'

xt Hrw, mdw Hr-rp.f, mryw nb.f, pw tri rf sw

following Horus, speak on-behalf-of.him, desire/wish lord.his, who pray then it?

'the following of Horus, who speaks on his behalf what his lord desired, who pray then is it?

imsti Hpy dwA-mwt.f qbH-snw.f, inD-Hr.tnw

Imseti Hapy Duamutef Qebehsenuef, hail-to.you

'It is, Imseti, Hapy, Duamuted and Qebehsenuef, hail to you'

nbw mAat, DADAt, HA-tp, Awsir, didyw, Sadw

lords truth/justice, magistrates, behind/around, Awsir, causing terror/cut-down

'lord of justice, magistrates behind Osiris, causing to put terror'

m isfAt, imyw xt Htp, Htp-s-xw.s

into wrong-doings, those-who-are-in following-after,
pacify-make-protected.her (goddess Hetep-Sekhu.s)

**'into those doing wrong, who are following after Her, Hetep-Sekhus, the goddess,
who satisfies and makes protected'**

ma.tnw, wi ii, kwi xr.tnw, dr.tn, Dwt nb

give.you I, come I under.you, drive-out.you, evil all

'you give I, that I may come to you, that you may drive out all evil'

iryw.i, mi nnw, ir n.tnw, n Axw 7

relating-to.me, like those, do of.you, for glorified-spirits 7

'relating to me like that which you did for those seven glorified Akh-spirits'

ipw imyw, Smsw, n nb.snw, spA
these who-are-in followers, of lord.their, Sepa
'these who are in the followers of their lord, Sepa'

Sepa: was a centipede god from Heliopolis with the powers to prevent snake bites. He could also be represented with the head of a donkey or as a mummiform deity sporting two short horns.

ir n inpw, st.s(nw), hrw pwy, n miy, irk im
made of Inpw (Anubis), place.their, day that, of come now therein
'Anubis made their places on that day of Come-Now-Therein'

pw tri rf sw, ir nn, nbw mAawt, DHwty pw
who pray then it? as-to these, lords justice, Thoth it-is
'who pray then is it? as to these Lords of Justice, it is Thoth'

Hna isds, nb imntt, ir DADAt, HA-tp Awsir

with Isdes, lord west, as-to magistrates, behind Osiris

'with Isdes (Judge of the Dead), Lord of the West, as to the magistrates who are behind Osiris'

imsti, Hpy, dwA-mwt.f, qbH-snw.f

Imseti, Hapy, Dua-mut.ef, Qebeh-senu.ef

'Imseti, Hapy, Duamutef, Qebehsenuef'

nA pw nty, m-sA, pA xpS, m pt mHtt

these it-is who, in back, the Thigh, in heaven northern

'these it is who are in the back of the Thigh (Ursa Major) in the Northern Heavens'

Four of the Seven Glorious Akh-Spirits: The Seven magistrates are represented by the seven stars of the northern constellation, Ursa Major, known by the early and pre-dynastic Egyptians as the Thigh. Those at the back of the Thigh are the Four sons of Horus who represent the four cardinal points, north, south, east and west, where each one is represented by the four bright stars in the pan shaped box at the top of the Thigh constellation, namely the stars known as Merak, Megrez, Phad and Dubhe.

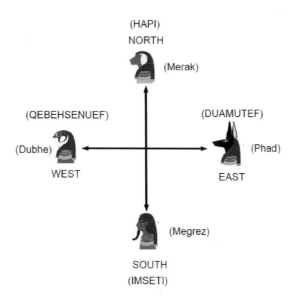

The seven stars of the Thigh constellation of which four were the Sons of Horus are the Imperihable circumpolar stars, the stars which never set, the eternal Akh-Spirits:

𓀀𓏤𓃀𓏏𓏏𓇼𓇼𓇼 **ixmw-skw** 'the indestructable stars'

 [hieroglyphic text]
ir ddyw Sad, m isftw, imiw xt, Htp-s-xyw.s
as-for putting terror/cut-down, into wrong-doers, those-who-in following, pacify-make-protected.she
'as for terror into the wrong doers, who are in the following of Her, the Goddess, Hetep-Sekhu, She who satisfies and makes protected'

[hieroglyphs]

sbk pw, imy mw, ir Htp-s-xwy, irt pw, nt ra

Sobek it-is, those-who-are-in waters, as-for goddess-Hetep-Sexwy, eye it-is of Ra

'it is Sobek and those who are in the Waters, as for She, the Goddess Hetep-Sekhui, who Satisfies and makes protected, she is the Eye of Ra'

[hieroglyphs]

ky Dd, nsrt wnn.s, m-xt Awsir, Hr sAmt

another saying: flame exists.she, following-after Osiris, upon burning-up

'another saying, she is the Flame which follows after Osiris, on burning up'

[hieroglyphs]

bA nw xftyw.f, ir Xrt Dwt nb, iry Awsir sS

souls of enemies.his, as-to concerning evil all, relating-to Osiris scribe

'the souls of his enemies, as to concerning all the evil relating to the Osiris Scribe'

Htp-nTr, n nTrw nbw, Anwy, mAa-xrw, Dr hAy.f, m Xt, n mwt.i

offering-divine, of gods all, Anwy, true-voice, since go-down, from womb, of mother.my

'of the Divine Offering of all the gods, Anwy, True of Voice,
since I came down from my mother's womb'

---

ir Xrt, Axw pw, 7, imsti, Hpy, dwA-mwt.f

as-to concerning, glorified-Akh-spirits, 7, Imseti, Hapy, Duamutef

'as for the seven glorified Akh-spirits, Imseti, Hapy, Duamutef'

---

qbH-snw.f, mAA-it.f, Xry-bAq.f, Hrw-xnty-mAA-two

Qebeh-snu.f, Maa-it.f, Khery-baq.f, Horus-Khenty-Maawy

'Qebeh-senu-ef, Maa-it-ef, Khery-baq-ef, Horus-khenty-maawy'

Hieroglyphs	Phonetic Spelling	Translation	Name (goddess)
	im-sti	One Who is in it	Imseti (Isis)
	Hpy	One who Proceeds by Boat	Hapy (Nephthys)
	dwA-mwt.f	He who Adores His Mother	Dua-mut-ef (Neith)
	qbH-senw-ef	One who Libates His Brothers	Qebeh-senu-ef (Serket)
	mAA-it.f	He who Sees His Father	Maa-it-ef
	Xry-bAq.f	He who is under the Moringa Tree	Khery-baq-ef
	Hrw-xnty-irwy Her-xnty-mAAwy	Horus Foremost Eyes* Horus Foremost Seer	Heru-khenty-irwy Heru-khenty-maaui

* Some translate his name as: Horus the Eyeless?

rdit.snw, in inpw, m sAw, qrs nt Awsir, ky Dd
place by.they, by Inpw, as protectors, burial of Osiris, another saying:
'they are placed by Anubis as the protectors of the burial of Osiris, another way saying'

Upper Register

Falcon, the Soul of Ra, wearing the sun disk facing a Ba Bird, the soul of Osiris wearing the White Crown of Upper Egypt between Two Djed Pillars (Djedw, Busiris). A Cat, the Sun, sitting beneath the Ished Tree of Life in Heliopolis cutting off the head of the Apep serpent. Three seated dieties holding knives. Ani and his wife Tutu who holds a sistrum both kneeling in adoration of the god Khepri in his solar bark. The beetle headed god Khepri in his bark represents the rising sun. Two baboons with arms raised worshipping the rising sun. The god Temu ⟨glyph⟩ seated within the sun in his bark of the setting sun. The recumbent lion god Rhu. The serpent Wadjet, Lady of the Flame, Eye of Ra coiled around a lotus flower with the emblem of Fire ⟨glyph⟩.

⟨hieroglyphs⟩
m-sA wabt, nt Awsir, ky Dd, ir Axw, 7, ipw
at-back embalming-place, of Osiris, another saying, as-for Akh-spirits, 7, these
'behind the Embalming Place of Osiris, another saying: as for these seven Glorified Akh-spirits'

⟨hieroglyphs⟩
nDH-nDH, iA-qd-qd, n-rdi-n.f-bsw.f-xnty-nty-hh.f
Nedjeh-Nedjeh, Ia-qed-qed, to/for-place-for.him-flame.his-front-of-blast of fire.his
'Nedjeh-Nedjeh, Ia-qed-qed, one who placs his flame for him at the front of his blast of fire'

aq-Hr-imy-wnwt.f, dSr-irty, imy-Hwt-insy

enter-upon-who-is-in-hour.his, red-eyes, who-is-in-mansion-bright-red-linen

'one who enters to he, in his hour, Red-Eyes, who is in the Mansion of Bright Red Linen'

---

bsw-Hr-pr-m-xt-xt, mAA-m-grH-ini.n.f-m-hrw

flame-one-upon-come-out-after-turning-back, see-in-night-bring.of-to.him-in-day

**'Flaming One who comes out after turning back,
one who sees in the night that which he brings in the day'**

---

ir Hry DADAwt, n nA, Iry.f, Hrw nD, Hr it.f

as-to chief magistrates, of this, hall.his, Horus protect, upon father.his

'as to the Chief of these Magistrates, Horus protected his father'

ir Xrt hrw pf imay.i, irk im, Dd Awsir pw, n ra

as-to concerning, day that, come-to.i, then therein, speak Osiris it-is, to Ra

'as to concerning that day of 'Come to me,' then therein it is Osiris speaking to Ra'

imy irk im, mAA.tw, xrw.fy.st.i, r imntt

come now therein, see.you, say.it.me, to west

'come now therein, that I may see you, I said it in the West (Imentet)'

ink bA.f, Hr-ib TA.fy, pw tri rf sw, Awsir pw

I soul.his, in-heart-of fledgling-dual, who pra then he? Osiris it-is

'I am his soul in the heart of the Two Fledglings, who pray then is he? he is Osiris'

aq.f, r Ddw, gm.n.f, bA, im n ra

enter.he, to Djedu, found.of.him, soul, therein of Ra

'when he entered into Mendes (Djedet), he found the soul therein of Ra'

aHa.n, Hpt n ky, im, aHa.nw, xpr m bAw, TA.fy

listen, embrace of another, therein, listen, come-into-existence of souls in-heart-of fledglings.dual

**'listen, they embraced each other therein, listen, there came into existence
the souls in the heart of the Twin Fledglings'**

The following text has been accidently ommitted by the scribe of the Amwy papyrus, but is here supplied from that of Nebseni:

ir TA.fy, Hr pw, nD Hr it.f

as-for fledglings-dual, Horus it-is, protection of father.his

'as for the Two Fledglings, it is Horus, the protector of his father'

(hieroglyphs)
Hna Hrw-m-xnt-n-mAA, ky Dd, bA.fy Hr-iby, TA.fy
with Horus-as-foremost-of-seeing, another saying: souls-dual upon-heart, fledglings dual
'with Herw-em-xent-en-maa, another way of saying, the Twin Ba-souls in the midst of the Two Fledglings'

(hieroglyphs)
bA pw, n ra, bA pw, n Awsir pw, n imi Sw
soul it-is, of Ra, soul it-is, of Osiris it-is, of which-is-in Shu
'the soul it is of Ra, the soul it is of Osiris, of which is in Shu'

(hieroglyphs)
bA pw, n imi nwt, bA.fy pwy, n imiw Ddt
soul it-is, of which-is-in Nut, soul-dual it-is, of which-is-is Djedet
'the soul it is of which is in the goddess Nut, the Twin Souls it is which is in Djedet (Mendes)'

Mendes: the Greek name of the Ancient Egyptian city of Djedet, also known in Ancient Egypt as Per-Banebdjedet (Domain of the Ram Lord of Djedet) and Anpet, is known today as Tell El-Ruba.

ink miw pwy, pSny iSd, r-gs.ff, m iwnnw, grH pwy

I-am cat that, split-in-two Ished-tree to-side.its, in Heliopolis, night that

'I am the Cat that split in two the Ished Tree (Persea Tree, Tree of Life) to its side in Heliopolis on that night'

n Htm xftyw, nw nbr-dr, im.f, pty tri rf sw

of destroying enemies, of Neb-er-Djer, therein.it, what pray then it/

'of destroying the enemies of Neb-er-Djer (Lord to End) therein it, what pray then is it?'

miw pwy, ra pw Dsf, Dd.tw, n.f, miw, m Dd siA, r.f

cat that, Ra it-is him-self, spoke.one, for.him, when Sia, about.him

'that Cat is it Ra himself, when Sia spoke about him'

miw m nn, ir.n.f, xpr rn.f, pw, n miw, ky Dd

cat-like in that, did.of.he, become name.his, it-is, of Cat, another saying:

'he was cat-like in that he did and became his name it is of Cat, another saying'

wnn Sw pw, Hr irt, imt n gb, n Awsir

be Shu it-is, upon doing, inventory/property for Geb and Awsir

'it will be Shu making inventory for Geb and Osiris'

ir Xr pSn, inD, r-gs.f, m iwnnw, wn msw, bdSt pw

as-to concerning splitting, Ished-tree, to-side.its, in Heliopolis, happen-when children, impotent, it-is

'as to concerning the splitting of the Ished Tree to its side in Heliopolis, it happened when the Impotent (faint/weary) Children it is'

Hr mAa, Hr ir.n.snw, ir Xrt grH pf, aHA, aq.snw pw

upon justice, because did.of.them, as-to concerning night that, fight, enter.they it-is

'for justice concerning what they did, as to that night of fighting, they entered it is'

---

m iAbty pt, aHa.n, a n aHA, m pt, m tA, r Dr.f

in eastern heaven, listen-to-this, region of fighting, in heaven, in earth, to end.its

'in the eastern heaven, listen, the region of battle, was in heaven and in the earth to its end'

---

i imi swHt.f, psd m itn.f, wbn m Axt

hail who-is-in egg.his, shining from Sun-disk.his, appearing in horizon

'hail who is in his egg, shining from his Sun Disk, appearing in the horizon'

Egg of Ra: is a common element in Egyptian cosmogonies and a substitute for the primeval waters or the primeval mound.

nbi Hr biA, nty nw-sn.f, m nTrw, sqdd Hr sTsw

swiming over the heavens, not second.he, among gods, sailing over supports-Shu

**'swimming over the heavens, he is not second among the gods
sailing over the Supports of Shu'**

didi nfw, m hh, n (rA).f, s-HD tAwy, m Axw.f

giving breath of fire, of mouth.his, make-bright two-lands, with sunshine.his

'giving the breath of fire of his mouth, making bright the Two-Lands with his sunshine'

nHm.k, nb-sny, nb imAx nTr pwy, StA irw

save.you, Neb-seny, lord venerated, god that, secret form

'may you save Neb-seny, the venerated lord, that god of secret form'

wnn inH.fy, m awy maXAt grH pfy, Hsbt awA

exist eyebrows, as arms balance, night that, reckoning robbing-goddess

whose eyebrows exist as the arms of the balance, that night of the Thief Goddess'

---

pty tri rf sw, in-a-f, pw, ir Xrt grt pf

who pray then it? In-a-ef, it-is, as-to on night that

'who pray then is he? In-a-ef (Brings-His-hand) it is, as to on that night'

---

n- Hsbt awA, grH pw, n nsrt, n xryt

of reckoning thief-goddess, night it-is, of flame-goddess, of fallen

'of reckoning of the Thief-Goddess, it is the night of the Flame-Goddess of the enemy'

didi s-rHw, m isft, r nmt.f, dnd bAw

give make-battle, of wrong-doers, in slaughter-house.his, slaughter souls

'cause to make battle with the wrongdoers in his slaughter house, slaughtering souls'

pty tri rf sw, Ssmw pw, sidy pw, n Awsir

who pray then he, Shesmu it-is, slaughterer it-is, of Osiris

'who then pray is he? he is Shesmu, he is the slaughterer of Osiris'

Shesmu: is the ancient Egyptian god of execution, slaughter, blood, oil, wine and perfume.

ky Dd, aA-pp pw, wn.n.f, m tp n wa, Xrt mAat

another say, Aa-pep it-is, be.he, with head of one, under righteousness

'another way of saying, it is the Aa-pep serpent, when he has one head under righteousness'

ky Dd, Hrw pw, wn n.wa, m tpyw, wn.n wa Xrt mAat, ky Xr isft

another say, Horus it-is, when.of.he, with heads-two,
when of.one under righteousness, one under wrong

'another saying, it is Horus when he has two heads,
one having righteousness, one possessing wrong-doing'

didi.f, isft n ir.sy, mAat n Smsy, Xr.s, ky Dd

gives.he, wrongdoing for doer-of-it, righteousness for follower, possessing.it, another saying

'he gives wrongdoing for the doer of it
and righteousness for the follower possessing it, another saying'

Hrw pw, aA xnt, nt xm, DHwty pw, ky Dd, nfr-tm pw

Horus it-is, great foremost, of Khem (Letopolis), Thoth it-is, another say, Nefer-tem it-is

'it is Horus, great foremost of Khem, It is Thoth, another saying, it is Nefer-tem'

spdw xsf xt, n xftyw, nw nb-r-Dr, nHm.k

Soped drive-away things, of enemies, of Neb-er-Djer, take-away.you

'Soped, drive away things of the enemies of Neb-er-Djer (Lord to End), you deliver'

---

ma nn, n irw, stAw imnHy [ ] spdw DbA, mrw

from those, of whose-duty, deal-out wounds [ ] sharp fingers painful

'from those whose duty is to deal out wounds [with] painful sharp fingers'

Hsq imw, xt Awsir, nn sxm.snw, im.i, nn hAy.i

cut-off-head who-are-in, following Osiris, not power.they, in.me, not go-down.i

'those who cut off the heads of those who follow Osiris, they shall not have power over me, I shall not fall down'

rkwt, pty tri rf sw, inpw pw, Hrw m xnt, n irwy

to knives (their), who pray then it? Anubis it-is, Horus as foremost, of Two-Eyes

'to their knives, who pray then is it? it is Horus as the foremost of the god of Two Eyes'

ky Dd, DADA pw, xsft xt, n xf[tyw?].sn, [r-nbr-Dr?], ky Dd

another say, magistrates it-is, repel things of [enemies].their, [against Lord-to-End] another say

**'another saying, the magisrates it is, the repulsers of the things
of their [enemies against the Lord to End]'**

wr-Snayw, n Snayw, m sxm Ds.snw m......

great repeler-one?, of the repeler-house?, not power knives.their ...... over [me]

'the Great Repeler of the House of Replers? may their knives not have power......over [me]'

nn hAy, r ktwt.snw, Hr-ntt, twi rx kwi, rn

not fall, to knives.their, upon-that, I, know I, name

'may I not fall to their knives, because I, I know the name'

---

iry rx kwi, maDdt twy, imi.snw, n pr Awsir, stit m irt

as-to know I, oppressor that, among.them, of house Osiris, shoot eye

'as to I know the oppressor that who is among them of the house of Osiris, who shoots the eye'

---

n mAA ntwf, dbn n pt, ns n r(A).f, smi Hapy

not see he, go-around of heaven, flame of mouth.his, make report Hapy

'he is not seen, the flame of his mouth goes around the heavens, Hapy makes report'

m mAA ntw.f, ink wDA, tp tA, xr ra, mni.i, nfr xr Awsir

not see of.he, I prosperous, on earth, before Ra, die.i, happy before Osiris

'he is not seen, I was prosperous on Earth before Ra and I died happy before Osiris'

nn iabt,Tnw, im.i, nn, m Hrw, axw.snw, Hr ntt twi, m Smsw

not offering.your, into.i, those in above, brazier/altar.their, upon that I, in followers

'your offerings will not be through me, those who over their altar, because I in the followers'

n nb-r-Dr, r sSw, n xprw, aXA.i, m bik

of lord-to-end, at writings, of Khepri, fly.i, as falcon

'of the Lord-to-End' at the writings (edicts) of Khepri, I fly as a falcon'

ngg.n.i, m smn, ski.i, HH, mi nHb-kAw

cackle.i, as goose, pass-time.i, eternity, like uniter-souls (Neheb-kaw)

'I cackle as a goose, I pass time eternal, like Neheb-khaw, the Uniter of Souls'

pty tri st, nnw n Hrw, axw.snw, twt pw, n irt ra

what pray it? those of over (in charge), braziers.their, image it-is, of eye Ra

**'what pray is it? it is those who are in charge of their offering braziers,
it is the image of the Eye of Ra'**

Hna twt, n irt Hrw, i ra-tm, nb hwt-aAt, ity, anx, wDA, snb

together-with image, of eye Horus, hail Ra-Atum, lord temple-great,
sovereign, life, prosperity, health

**'and the image of the Eye of Horus, hail, Ra-Atum, lord of the Great Temple, sovereing, Life,
Prosperity and Health'**

[hieroglyphic line]

nTrw nbw, nHm.k, ma nTr pwy, nty Hr.f, m Tsm

gods all, deliver.you, from god that, who face.his, as hound

'of all the gods, you deliver me from that god, who, his face is as a hound'

[hieroglyphic line]

inH.fy, m rmT, anx.f, m xryt, sAw qAb, n S, n xt

eye-brows.his, as people, lives.he, by butchery, guards interior, of lake, of fire

'whose his eye-brows are as people, he lives by butchery guarding the lake of fire'

[hieroglyphic line]

am XAt, xnp HAtw, wdd sTA, n mAA ntw.f

swallows corpse, steals hearts, inflicts-injury odour, not see of.him

'who swallows the corpse, steals hearts and inflicts injury and odours, while unseen'

ptr rf sw, am HH, rn.f, wnn m iAt, ir Xrt iAt, n xt

who pray then he? swallower millions, name.his, exist in mound,
as-to concerning mound, of fire

'who pray then is he? the Swallower of Millions, is his name, he dwells in the Mound, as to concerning the Mound of Fire'

pA pw, nty, r imy.tw, ny-ni-rwd-rf r Snyw

this it-is, which, at in.one, Naref to entourage-court

'this it is which is in between Naref and the Court of the Enourage

Naref: a place in Heracleopolis (Early Dynastice Town, 20th Nome) where Osiris was buried

ir xnd nb, Hr.(f) sAwt, xr.f, n Safw

as-to tread any, upon.(it) beware/guard fallen.he, to knives

'as to anyone who treads upon it, beware he shall fall to the knives

ky Dd, mds rn.f,iry-aA pw, n imnt, kyy-Dd, bAbA rn.f

another say, sharp-of-knife name.his, guard-door it-is, of west, Ba-ba? name.his

'another saying, Sharp of Knife his name, door-keepr of the West, Ba-Ba his name'

nt.f sAw qAb pwy, n imntt, ky Dd, Hry-sp, rn.f

of.he/belongs-to-him, guradian interior that, of west, another say, chief-time, name.his

'of he who is the guardian of that interior of the West, another saying, Hery-Sep his name'

i, nb nriw, Hry-tp tAwy, nb dSrt, wAD nmiwt

O lord terror, chief two-lands, lord blood, flourish slaughter-blocks

'O lord of terror, Chief of the Two Lands, flourishing slaughter blocks' anx m bskw, pty tri rf sw, sAA qAb pwy, imntt

live on entrails, who pray then it? guardian interiour that, west

'who lives on entrails, who then pray is it? it is the guradian of that interior of the West'

---

pty tri rf sw, HAty pw, n Awsir, ntf wnm, Sat nb

who pray then is-he, heart it-is, of Osiris, and.he eats slaughtered-things all

'who pray then is he? he is the heart of Osiris and he devours all slaughtered things'

---

rdy n.f, wrrt, Aw-ib, m xnt, Hnn-nswt, pty tri rf sw

give to.him, white-crown, happy, as foremost child-royal-city, who pray then is he?

'and was given to him the Werret (Great White) Crown and joy, foremost in Heracleopolis. who pray then is he?'

ir rdy n.f, wrrt, Aw-ib, m xnt Hnn-nswt, Awsir pw

as-to given to.him, great-crown, joy, as foremost city-royal-child, Osiris it-is

'as to it is given to him the Great Crown and joy as foremost in Henen-Newswt, it is Osiris'

---

wdd.f, HqAt, m nTrw, hrw pf, smAt tAwy, m-bAH a nb-r-Dr

command.he, rule, among gods, day that, of unite two-lands, in-presence-of hand lord-to-end

'he was commanded to rule that day among the gods of uniting the Two Lands in the presence of the hand of Neb-er-Djer, Lord of Entirety'

---

pty tri rf sw, ir wdd n.f, HqAt m nTrw, Hrw pw, sA ist

what pray then it? as-to command to.him, rule among gods, Horus it-is, son Isis

'what pray then is is? as to concerning the command to him ,
rule among the gods, Horus, son of Isis'

s-HqA m st, it.f Awsir, ir hrw pf, smAt tAwy, dmd tAwy, pw r

made-rule in throne, father.his, Osiris, as-to day that union two-lands, unite two-lands, it-is at

'who was made to rule in the place of his father Osiris on that day of the union of the Two Lands, the union of the Two Lands it is at'

---

qrs Awsir, bA anx, imy nswt-Hnn, rdi kAw

burial Osiris, living ram, who-is-in royal-child-city, gives food

'the burial of Osiris, living ram, who is in Heracleopolis. who gives food'

---

dr isft, sSm.n.f, wat HH, pty tri rf sw, ra pw Ds.f

drive-out wrongdoing guide.of.he, way eternal, what pray then is-it?

'and drives out evil, he guides the eternal way, what pray then it?'

ra pw, nHm.k, xr nTr aA, pwy, TAy bAw, nsbw iwA

Ra it-is, rescue.you, under god great, that, seizes souls, lick-up corruption?

'Ra it is, you rescue before the great god that seizes souls and licks up corruption'

anx m HwAyt, sA kkw, imy snkt, snDw.f

living on decay, guardian darkness, which-is-in darkness/obscurity, fear.him

'living on decay, guardian of darkness which is in obscurity, fear him'

imyw bg, pty tri ef sw

who-is-in weakness, who pray then it?

'those who are in weakness, who pray then is it?'

ir Xrt bAw, Hr-ib, TAy.f ma nTr pwy, TAy bA.i

as-to concerning souls, within, save.you from god that, seize soul

'as to concerning souls within you save from the god that seizes the soul'

nsbw HAtw, anx m HwAw, iry kkw

laps-up hearts, lives on corruption, thereof guardian darkness

'who laps up hearts, who lives on corruption, thereof the guardian of darkness'

imy skry snD n.f, imyw bgAw

those-who-in Sekery-boat, fear of.him, those-who-in slack/remiss

'those who among the Sekery Boat, fear him, those who are slack'

[hieroglyphs]
pw tri rf sw, swty pw, ky- Dd, smA-wr
who pray then he? Seth it-is, another saying: wild-bull-great
'who pray then is he? it is Seth, another way of saying, the Great Wild Bull'

[hieroglyphs]
bA n gb, i xpri, Hr-ib wiA.f, pAwt Dt.f
soul of Geb, hail Khepri, in-midst boat.his, primeval-time-dual, body.his
'soul of Geb, hail Khepri, in the midst of his boat, the double primeval time his body'

[hieroglyphs]
nHm.k, Awsir Anwy, maA-xrw, mA nnw pw, iryw sipw
save.you, Osris Anwy, true-voice, from those it-is, guardians inspection-ones
'you save Osiris Anwy, True of Voice, from those it is the guardians who examine'

rdi.n.snw, nb-r-Dr, r Axw n.f, r irt-sAtw xftyw.f

given.of.they Neb-er-Djer, to godly-power for.him, do-guard enemies.his

'they are given by the Lord of All, godly power to guard against his enemies'

---

didyw Sad, m iAty, ntyw pr, m sAtw.snw

place knives, in slaughter-houses, who-do-not come-forth, from guardianship.their

'who put knives into the slaughter houses, who do not leave from their guardianship'

---

nn hAby.snw, ds.snw, im.i, nn aq.i, r iAty.snw

not send.they, knives.their, into.me, not enter.i, slaughter-houses.their

'they shall not send their knives into me, I shall not enter their slaughter houses'

nn wrd.n.i, m Xnw, smAwt.snw

not weary.of.i, in interior, killing-chambers.their

'I shall not fail inside their killing chambers'

---

nn irtw n.i, xt m nnw, bwt nTrw, Hr nty, ink wab, Hr msqt

not done to.me, things from those, hate gods, upon which, I bathed, upon Milky-Way

'nothing shall be done to me from those which hate gods, I am bathed upon the Milky Way'

---

ini.n.f, msy m tiHnt, imi tAnnt, pw tri rf sw

bring to.me, supper of faience, withing Tanenet-shrine, what pray then it?

'brought to me a supper of faience within the Tanenet Shrine.* what pray then is it?'

* Tomb of Osiris

[hieroglyphic line 1]

xpri Hr-ib wiA.f, ra pw Ds.f, ir nnw, n iryw sipw

Khepri in-midst boat.his, Ra it-is self.him, as-to those, of guardians, of inspected

**'it is Khepri in the midst of his boat, it is Ra himself,
as to those guardians who are to be inspected'**

[hieroglyphic line 2]

bntt pw, st pw, nb-hwt pw, ir nnw, n bwt nTrw

apes it-is, Isis it-is, Nephthys it-is, as-to those, of hate gods

'apes it is, Isis it is, Nephthys it is, as to those who the gods hate'

[hieroglyphic line 3]

Hsw pw, grg, ir sS, wabt, Hr-ib, msqt, inpw pw

excretement it-is, falsehood, as-to pass, bathed, in-midst, Milky-Way, Anubis it-is

**'excretement it is and falshood, as to those who passed on the midst
of the Milky Way, Anubis it is'**

iw.f, m sA, afdt, ntt Xr maXwt, n Awsr, ir rdyt n.f

is.he, as behind chest, which under entrails, of Osiris, as-for giving to.him

'he is as behind the chest which contains the entrails of Osiris, as for giving to him

---

msyt m tiHnt, im tAnnt, Awsir pw, ky Dd

supper of faience, in Tanenet, Osiris it-is, another saying

a supper of faience in Tanenet (the Shrine of Osiris), it is Osiris, another saying,

---

ir msyt, m tiHnt, imw tA-nnt, pt pw, tA pw

as-for supper, of faience, in Tanenet-shrine, heaven it-is, earth it-is

'as for the supper of faience in the Shrine of Tanenet, it is Heaven and it is Earth'

ky Dd, qnqn Sw, nt tAwy pw, m nswt-Hnn, ir msyt

another say: hammer-out Shu, of two-lands it-is, in Heracleopolis, as-for supper

**'another saying, it is that Shu hammered out the Two Lands in Heracleopolis,
as for the supper'**

m tiHnt, irt Hrw pw, ir tA-nnt, smAt pw, nt Awsir

of faience , eye Horus it-is, as-for Ta-enenet, tomb it-is, of Osiris

'of faience, it is the Eye of Horus, as for the Tanenet Shrine, it is the Tomb of Osiris'

qd pr.k, tmw, snT Hwt.k, rw-rw-ti pH, n pXrt, twri Hrw

build house.your, Atum, founded mansion.your, Ru-ru-ti arrive, turn, show-respect-to Horus

**'build your house, Atum founded your Mansion, the Two Lions, arrive and turn to,
show respect to Horus'**
ʼ

nTry st, Ts-pXr, ii.n.f, m tA pn, iTi.n.f, m rdwy.f

divine Seth, arrange-around, come.of.he, to land this, seize.of.he, with two-feet.his

'Seth divine, and vice-versa, he came to this land and he seized it with his two feet'

Awsir sS Anwy, maA-xrw, xr Awsir, nt.f, tmw, iw.f, m niwt.k

Osiris scribe Anwy, true-voice, under Osiris, of.he, Atum, is.he, in town.your

'Osiris Scribe Anwy, True of Voice under Osiris, he is Atum, he is in your town'

HA-tp.k, sw ir sAw, nn mAA.tw.f, sAwty

turn-back.you, him do/act guard, not see.of.one.him, guardian

'you turn back, he acts as guard, one does not see him, the guardian'

Awsir Anwy, ntf st, gmt n.f, sw, psx.f, Sny n Hr.f

Osiris Anwy, of.him Isis, found.of.he, him, disarranged.he, hair of face.his

'Osiris Anwy, he is Isis, he found him, he disarranged the hair of his face'

txtx r wpt, iw-wr n.f, m ist, bnn n.f, m nb-hwt

disorder.i, to brow, become-pregnant of.he, in Isis, beget of.he, in Nephthys

'I disordered my brow, Isis became pregnant with him, Nephthys begat him'

bHnn.snw, Xnnw.f, rnw m-xt.k

cut-off/drive-off.they, disturb.him, dread/fear follows-after.you

'they drive off who disturbs him, dread follows after you'

SfSft.k, tp awy.f, qaH.k, r HHw, rmnw.snw

respect/awe.your, on arms-two.his, bend.you, to millions, arms.their

'your respect is upon his two arms, millions bend their arms to you'

pXr n.k, rxwt sxbxbt.k, wnDwt xftyw.k

turn-around to.you, common-folk, make-destroyed.you, associates enemies.your

'you turn around the common folk to you, you destroy the associates of your enemies'

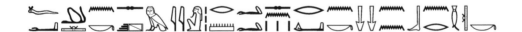

kfa n.k, siAmy rmnwy.snw, rdi.n.k, snsn bnr.k

uncover.of.you, grey-haired-ones? arms.their, give to.you, well-disposed pleasant.you,

'the grey-haired ones uncover their arms for you, the well disposed are pleasant to you'

qmA.k, imy SfSft.k, imy Xr-aHA, imy iwnnw nTr nb

create.you, who-is-in Kher-Aha, those-in Iunnw, god every

'you create those who are in Kher-Aha and those who are in Heliopolis, every god'

snD.n, n.k wrt aA, SfSft.k, nTr nb, ma s-Hrwi sw

fear.of to.you, very great, respect/awe.you, god any, cause-vilify him

'fears you, every god respects you and causes to vilify him'

stt sn, anx.k, r mry.k, ntk wADyt, nbt imw xt

shoot shrine? live.you, to desire.your, you Wadet, lady in flame

'shooting the shrine, you live according to your desire, you are Wadet, Lady within the Flame'

ary.snw, n.k, and im.snw, pw tri rf sw, StA irw

rise-up.they, against.you few-people among.them, what pray then it? secret forms

'they rise up against you, the few people amongst them, what pray then is it? secret forms'

didi mnHw, rn n HAd/HAt, mAA.tw.f, Hr a rn

given Menhu, name of tomb, see.one.his, upon hand name

'given Menhu, the name of the tomb, he sees one upon the hand, the name'

n qriw, ky Dd, rn n nmt, ir sA HD, r psd tp

of storm-cloud, another say: name of slaughter-house, as-to back? bright, mouth moveable? head

**'of the storm cloud, another saying, the name of the slaughter house,
as to the shining mouth and moving head'**

Hnn pw Awsir, ky Dd, Hnn pw ra, ir psdx n.k, Sn.k

phallus it-is Osiris, another saying, phallus it-is of Ra, as-to disarrange toyou, hair.your

**'the phallus it is of Osiris, another saying, it is the phallus of Ra,
as for the disarranging of your hair'**

---

txtx.i n r wpt, wnn ist pw, Hr StA im.s, aHa-n.s, in n.s, Sny.s, im

disordered.i to brow, be Isis it-is, upon secret in.it, listen.she,
delay/hold aloof.of.it, hair.her, therein

'and disordered my brow, it is Isis who is secretly in it, listen, she holds aloof her hair therein'

---

ir wADy nbt, imw xt, irt ra pw

as-for Wadjy lady, who-is-in fire, eye Ra it-is

'as for Wadjyt, Lady of the Flame, it is the Eye of Ra'

aryt tp, rn iry-aA.s, sxd Hr, aSA irw, rn n sAty.s

gate/dwelling first, name of door-keeper.it, Inverted Face, Many Forms, name of guardian.its

**'The First Portal: the name of its door-keeper is Inverted Face,
Many Forms, the name of its guardian'**

mtty-ggi-HH, rn n smi, im.s, hA-xrw, Dd mdw in, Anwy maA-xrw

controller-stare-blast-fire?, name of announcer, in.it, go-down-voice,
spoken words by, Anwy true-voice

'Metty-Heh, the name of the announcer in it, Ha-kherw, Words spoke by Anwy, True of Voice'

xft spr, r aryt tpt, ink wr, ir sSp.f, ii.n.i, xr.k, Awsir

when arrive to portal first, I great, made light.his, come-forth.of.i, under.you, Osiris

**'when arriving at the First Portal, I am the Great One who made his light,
I come forth under you Osiris'**

dwA.i.you, wab r rSw.k, stA im.k, irwt rn

worship.i.you, purified from eflux-of-body.your, lead/drag/flow within.you, make name

'I worship you, purified by the eflux of your body which flows within you, make the name'

n r-sTAw, r.f, inD-Hr.k, Awsir m sxmw.k, wsrw.k, m r-sTAw

of Re-setjau, to.him, homage-upon.you, Osiris in might.your, power.your, in Re-setjau

'of Rosetjau to him, homage to you Osiris in your might and your power in Rosetjau'

Ts.tw, sxm.k, Awsir m iAbDw, pXr.k, pt. Xnt.k tw xft ra

raise.you, might.you, Osiris in Abydos, go-around.you, heaven, row.you, one before Ra

**'Raise yorself up in your might Osiris in Abydos,
you go around heaven sailing as one before Ra'**

mAA.n.k, rxyt nb, i pXr n ra, im.s, ma.k, Dd.i, Awsir, ink saH

see.of.you, common-people all, hail go-around for, in.it, say.i, I-am

'you see all the common people, hail, Ra goes around in it, I say Osiris I am a dignitary'

nTr, Dd.n.i, xpr nn xsf, Hr.s, m inb.f, Dabt wpt, m r-sTAw

god say.of.i, happens, not repulsed, upon.it, by wall.it, charcoal, open way in Re-setjau'

**'a god, I speak and it happens, I am not repulsed by it the wall of charcoal.
Open the way in Rosetjau'**

s-nDm mn Awsir, sxn nty wDa iAt, irt wAt.f, m int

made-comfortable sickness Osiris, embrace who cut-off-head standard, make way.his, in valley

**'cure the sickness of Osris, embrace the one who cut off the head of the standard,
who made his way in the valley'**

wr irt wAt sSp nt Awsir

great-one make way bright for Osiris

'Great one make the way bright for Osiris'

THE SECOND PORTAL

aryt sn, rn n iry-aA.s, wn-aA-HAt, rn sAwty.s, sqd-Hr

portal second, name of door-keeper.it, open-door-first, name guardian, Seqed-Herw

**'The second portal: the name of the door-guard, Wen-aa-hat,
name of the guardian Seqed-Herw'**

rn n smi, im.s, wsd, Dd mdw in, Awsir Anwy tn

name of anouncer, in.it, Wesed, spoken words by, Osiris Anwy this

'the name of the anouncer in it, Wesed, words spoken by this Osiris Anwy'

Hms.f, Hr irt tp, m xmt wDA, mdwt m sn, DHwty makt, DHwty

sit.he, upon doing in front three, judge words as second, Thoth protects Thoth

'he sits upon doing in front of the three, judgement of words, as second to Thoth, protector of Thoth'

m gH mAatA StA, anxwy m mAat, m rnpt.snw

not weary just-gods secret, who-live on truth, in years.their

'do not be weary secret gods of justice who live on truth in their years'

ink wdn At, irt wAt.f, iw xnd, ir n Hpt wAt

I weighty striking-power, makes way.his, is/are tread-ways, do seek-out way

'I am weighty of striking power, who makes his way, do seek out a way'

rdi.k, swAi Sd, mAA ra, ma iryw Htpw
give.you, pass rescue, see Ra, with who-makes offerings
'may you grant that I pass and rescue, may I see Ra among those who make offerings'

THE THIRD PORTAL

arywt xmt, rn n iry-aA, qq-HAwAtw-nt-pHwy
portal third, name of door-keeper, Qeq-Hawatu-net-Pehuy
'The Third Portal, the name of its door keeper, Qeq-Hawatu-net-Pehuy'

rn n sAyw.s, s-rs-Hr, rn n smi, im.s, aA
name of door-keeper.its, Ser-res-her (Watchful-Face), name of announcer, in.it, Aa (Door-Way)
'the name of its door-keeper, Ser-res-her, the name of the announcer in it, Aa'

Dd mdw in, Awsir Anwy, ink StA gb (gp-n-mw), wp r-Hwy
spoke words by, Osiris Scribe Anwy, I-am secret cloudburst, judge/divide two-combatants
'words spoken by the Osiris Scribe Anwy, I am the secret cloudburst who separated the Two Combatants (Horus and Seth)

ii n dr.i, Dwt Hr Awsir, ink wnx, At.f
come(.i) to drive-out, evil from Osiris, I-am clothed striking-power.his
'I have come to drive evil out from Osiris, I am clothed in his striking power'

pr m wrt, smnx.n.i, xt m AbDw, wp n wAt, m r-sTAw
come-forth in weret-crown, established.of.i, offerings in Abydos, open of way, in Re-setjau
'and come forth in the Weret Crown, I have established offerings in Abydos and opened the way in Rosetjau'

s-nDm n mnt, m Awsir, sxx iAt.f, ir.n.i, wAt sSp.f, m r-stAjw
eased-suffering of sickness, in Osiris, painted standard.his, do.of.i, way shine.he, in R-setau
'eased the suffering of the sickness in Osiris, painted his standard, I have made him shine in Rostjau'

THE FOURTH PORTAL

aryt fdw, rn n iry-aA.s, xsf-Hr-aSA-xrw
portal fourth, name of door-keeper.it, repel-face-many-voice
'The Fourth Portal, the name of its door-keeper, Khesef-Hr-asha-kheru'

rn n sAyt, s-rs-tpw, rn n smi, im.s, xsf-Ad
name of guardian, make-vigilant, name of anouncer, in.it, repel-crocodile
'the name of the guardian, Se-res-tepu, the name of its anouncer, Khesef-Ad'

Dd mdw, Awsir sS Anwy, mAa-xrw, ink kA, sA Dryt, nt Awsir
spoken words by, Osiris scribe Anwy, true-voice, I-am bull, son kite-bird, of Osiris
'words spoken by Osiris Scribe Anwy, True of Voice, I am the bull, the son of the Kite bird of Osiris'

ma.tnw, mtr n it.f, nb iAmw.f, wDa.n.i
give.you, witness of father.his, lord/possessor grave/charm.his, judged.of.i
'you give witness for his father, possessor of his charm, I judged'

bg(A)sw im, iw, ini.n, n.f, anx r fnd.f, n DtA
wrongdoing therein, is/are/behold, brought.of, to.him, life to nose.his, for eternity
'wrongdoing therein, behold I brought to him life to his nose for eternity'

ink sA Awsir, ir.n.i, wAt swAi.i, im, m Xrt-nTr

I-am son Osiris, made.of.i, way pass.i, therein, in under-god

'I am the son of Osiris, I made the way, I have passed therein into the Necropolis'

THE FIFTH PORTAL

aryt diw-nwt, rn n iry-aA.s, anx.f-m-fnt

portal fifth, name of door-keeper.its, lives-on-worms

'The Fifth Portal, the name of its door-keeper, Ankh.ef-em-fenet'

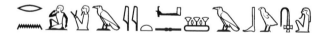

rn n sAyt.s, SAbw

name of guardian.it, Shabu

'the name of its guardian, Shabu'

rn n smi, im.s, db-Hr-khA-xft

name of anouncer, therein.it, hippopotomus-face-rage/bellow- in-front

'the name of its anouncer, Deb-her-kha-kheft'

Dd mdw in, Awsir sS Anwy, mAa-xrw, ini.n.i, arty imit r-sTAw

spoken words by, Osiris scribe Anwy, true-voice, brought.of.i, jaw-bone-dual therein Re-setjau

'words spoken by Osiris Scribe Anwy, True of Voice,
I have brought the two jawbones therein Rosetjau'

---

ini.n.i, n.k, psdw imi iwnnw, dmd aSA.f, im, xsf.i, n.k, aApp

brought.of.i, to.you, backbone therein Heliopolis, uniting many.his, therein, repel.i, for.you, Apep

'I have brought to you the backbone therein Heliopolis, uniting his many parts therein, I
repelled for you the Apep Serpent (Apophis)'

[hieroglyphs]

pgAs.n.i, nsp, iriw.n, wAt imy.tnw, ink smsw imt

spat.of.i, wounds, made.of, way among.you, I-am eledest among

'I spat upon the wounds and made a way among you, I am the eldest among'

PLATE 10: CHAPTER 147 continued

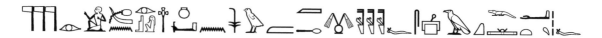

nTrw, ir.i, abw n Awsir, nD n sw, m maA-xrw, dmd qsw.f, sAqA at.f

gods, made.i, purifications for Osiris, save/protect of him, in triumph, unite bones.his, gathered limbs.his

'the gods, I have made puurifications for Osiris, protected him in triumph, united his bones and gathered his limbs'

THE SIXTH PORTAL

aryt sisw-nwt, rn n iry-aA.s, itk-tAw-khAq-xrw

portal sixth, name of door-keeper.its, seizer-of-bread-raise-voice

'The Sixth Portal, the name of its door-keeper, Itek-tau-khaq-kheru'

[hieroglyphs]
rn n sAyt.s, ini-Hr, rn n smi.s
name of guardian.its, brings-face, name of anouncer.its
'the name of its guardian, Ini-her, the name of its anouncer'

[hieroglyphs]
Ads-Hr-S, Dd mdw in, Awsir sS Anwy, ii.n.i, mi n hrw
sharp-face-lake, spoken words by, Osiris scribe Anwy, come-forth.of.i, like of day
'Ads-her-shw, spoke words by Osiris Scribe Anwy, I come forth like of day'

[hieroglyphs]
sp-sn, ir.n.i, wAt Smt.i, qmA n inpw, ink nb wrr
twice, do.of.i, way go/pass.i, create/begat of Anubis, I-am possessor Wereret-crown
'twice, I made the way, I passed that which begat Anubis, I am possessor of the Wereret Crown'

[hieroglyphs]

xmt HkAw, nD mAat, nD.n.i, irt sD.n.i, Awsir n.f

without magicians, protected truth, protected.of.i, eye, rescued.of.i, Osiris for.him

'without magicians, (I) protected truth, I protected the Eye (of) Osiris, I rescued for him'

[hieroglyphs]

iryw wAt Smt, Awsir Anwy, Hna.tnw im

made way passed, Osiris Anwy, together-with.you therein

'and made a way passed, Osiris Anwy, therein together with you'

THE SEVENTH PORTAL

aryt sfx-nw, rn n iry-aA.s, sxmt-dm(n)w.snw

portal seventh, name of keeper-door.its, power-over-knives.their

'The Seventh Portal: the name of its door-keeper, Sekhem-demw.senu'

rn sAyt.s, aA-mAa-xrw, rn n smi, n im.s

name guardian.its, great-true-voice, name of anouncer, of in.it

'the name of its guardian, Aa-maa-kheru, name of the anouncer in it'

xsf-xmyw, Dd mdw in, Awsir Anwy, ii.n.i, xr.k

repels-demolishers, spoken words by, Osiris Anwy, come.of.i, under/before.you

Khesef-khemyu, words spoken by Osiris Anwy, I come before you'

Awsir wab rDwt, pXr.k, pt, mAA.k, ra, mAA rxit wa

Osiris purified evils, go-around.you, heaven, see.you, Ra, see.you, common-people, sole-one

'Osiris, purified of evils, you go around the heavens, you see Ra,
you see the common people, O unique One'

is.k, m sktt, pXr.f, Axt nt pt, Dd.i, mrt.i, n saH.f

indeed.you, in night-bark, go-around.he, horizon of heaven, speak.i, wish.i, to dignity.his

'you indeed are in the Sektet Boat (Night Bark), he goes around the horizon of heaven, I speak what I desire to his dignity'

wsr.f, xpr.f, mi Dd.f, xsf.k, Hr.f, ir.n.i, wat nbt nfr, xr.k

powerful.he, create.it, like speak.he, repel.you, upon.he, make for.i, ways good all, before you

'his strength, it happens like as he speaks, you repel upon him, make for me all the good ways before you'

PLATE 11: UTTERANCE 146: THE FIRST GATEWAY

Ddwt, xft spr r sbxt, tpt, Dd mdw in, Awsir Anwy, mAa-xrw

said, when arrive/reach to gateway first, spoken words by, Osiris Anwy, true-voice

'Said when arriving to the First Gateway, words spoken by Osiris Anwy, True of Voice'

nbt stAw, qAt sbty, Hr-tp nbt, xbxbt

lady terror, high enclosure-walls, chief lady destruction

'Lady of Terror, the high enclosure walls, Chief Lady of Destruction'

---

rnt mdw, xsf nSny, nHm wAy, n iiy

name/proclaim words, repel rage/storms, take-away/rescue pludered-one, of coming-forth-one

'who proclaims words which repels storms, who rescues the plundered on who has come forth'

---

rn n iry-aA.s, nrwyt

name of gate-keeper.its, terror

'the name of its gate-keeper, Neruyt

Ddwt xft spr, r sbxt snw-nw, Dd mdw in, Awsir sS Anwy, maA-xrw, nb(t) pt, Hnwt tAwy

said when arriving, at gate-way second, spoken words bby, Osiris scribe Anwy, true-voice, lady heaven, mistress two-lands

'Said when arriving at the Second Gate-Way, words spoken by Osiris Scribe Anwy, True of Voice, Lady of Heaven, Mistress of the Two Lands'

nsbyt, nb(t) tmmt, tnwt, r bw-nbw

one-who-lap-up/devours, lady all-people, lift-up/promote/distinguish, more-than everyone

'the one who devours, Lady of Mankind, who distinguishes more than everyone'

rn n iry-aAw.s, ms-p(t)H pw

name of gate-keeper.its, Born-Ptah it-is

'the name of its gate-keeper, it is Mes-Ptah'

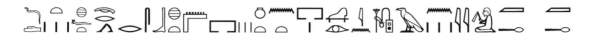

Ddwt xft spr, r sbxt xmt-nw, nt pr, Awsir Anwy, mAa-xrw...mAa-xrw

said when arriving, at gateway third, of house, Osiris Anwy, true-voice...true-voice

**'To be said when arriving at the Third Gateway, of the house of Osiris Anwy,
True of Voice...True of Voice'**

nbt xAwt, aAt abwt, smrt nTr nb, xnty iAbDw

lady altar, great offerings, cause-pain god any, sail-upstream Abydos

'Lady of the Altar of great offerings, who causes every god pain, who sails south to Abydos'

rn n iry-aA.s, sbAq

name of keeper-gate.its, splendid

'the name of its gateway-keeper, Sebaq'

Ddwt xft spr, r sbxt fdw-nw, in Awsir Anwy

said when arriving, at gateway fourth, (words spoken) by Osiris Anwy

'To be said when arriving at the Fourth Gateway, (words spoken) by Osiris Anwy'

sxm dsw, Hnwt tAwy, HDt xftyw, nw wrd-ib

power knives, mistress two-lands, destroy enemies, of weary-heart-one

**'Powerful of Knives, Mistress of the Two Lands, Destroyer of Enemies
of the Weary Hearted One'**

irt sArt, Sw m iw, rn n iry-aA.s, ngAw

doing wisdom, free/empty from wrong, name of keeper-gate, long-horned-bull

'doing wisdom the one free from wrong, the name of its gate-keeper, Negau'

Ddwt xft spr, r sbxt diw-nwt, in Awsr sS Anwy

words-said when arriving, at gateway fifth, by Osiris scribe Anwy

'Words to be said when arriving at the Fifth Gateway by Osiris Scribe Anwy'

xt nbt, HAw rSit, nn hA n sdbH.tw.s

fire lady, increase/excess joy, not go-down entreat.one.her

'Fire Lady, abundant joy, do not go down to entreat her'

nn aq, r.s, wnn tp.f, rn n iry-aA.s, Hnyt-ty-arqyw

not enter, to.her, be before.it, name of gate-keeper.its, spears-disaffected?-one

'do not enter to her to be before it, the name of its gate-keeper, Henetty-Areqyu'

Ddwt xft spr, r sbxt ssw-nwt, in Awsir sS Anwy

words-spoken when arriving, to gateway sixth, by Osiris scribe Anwy

'Words to be spoken when entering the Sixth Gateway by Osiris Scribe Anwy'

nbt snk, aAt hmhAt, n rx.tw, Awy.s, wsx.s, n gm.n.tw, qd

lady darkness, great shouting, not know.one, length.her, breadth.her, not find.of.one nature

'Lady of Darkness, great of shouting, one does not know her length and breadth, one has not found her nature'

m SAs, iw HfAw/Ddft Hr.s, nn rx, ms.n.tw, Xr Hat wrd-Hr

from beginning, is/are snakes upon.it, not know born.of.one, under front weary-one

'from the beginning, snakes are in it, one does not know who was begat before the Weary One'

[hieroglyphs]
rn n iry-aA.s, smAty
name of gate-keeper.its, united-one
'the name of its gate-keeper, Smaty'

[hieroglyphs]
Ddwt xft spr, r sxt sfxw-nwt, in Awsir sS Anwy, iAggyt
words-said when, entering gateway seventh, by Osiris scribe Anwy, veiling
'Words siad when entering the Seventh Gateway, by Osiris Scribe Anwy, veiling'

[hieroglyphs]
Hbst bgA
clothing feeble-one
'the clothes of the feeble one'

ikbyt mrr, sHAtp, rn iry-aA.s, ikty.f

weeping? wishes, conceal, name gate-keeper.its, Ikety.f

'weeping who wishes to conceal the name of its gate-keeper, Ikety.ef'

THE EIGHTH GATEWAY

Ddwt spr xft, r sbxt xmnw-nwt, in Awsir sS Anwy, mAa-xrw

words-said when entering, to gatewy eighth, by Osiris scribe Anwy, true-voice

'Words to be spoken when entering the Eighth Gateway by Osiris Scribe Anwy, True of Voice'

rkHt bsw, axm DAft, spdt patw, xAt dt

heat flame, extinguish/quench heat/burn, sharp flames, throw hand

'heat of flames, quencher of heat, sharp of flames, throwing hand'

smAt ntt nDnD, nty sS, Hr.s, n snD, nihy.s

kill/destroy not/without advice/counsel, not-one pass, upon.it, fear pain.hers

'who kills without warning, no one passes through it without her pain'

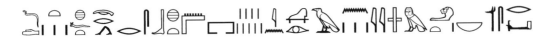

rn n iry-aA.s, xw-Dst.f

name of gate-keeper.its, protect-self.him

'the name of its gate-keeper, Khu-djest-ef'

THE NINTH GATEWAY

Ddwt xft spr, r sxt psDw, in Awsir Anwy, imi HAt, nb(t) wsr

spoken-words when entering, to gateway ninth, by Osiris Anwy, who-in front, lady power

'Words to be spoken when entering the Ninth Gateway by Osiris Anwy, one who is Foremost, Lady of Power'

hr(r)t/hrw-ib, msAwt, nb.s, xt 300+50, m DbAn/dbAn
content-hert, give-birth, lord.hers, rods 350, in girth (in circuit)
'Content of Heart, who gave birth to her lord, whose girth is 350 rods'

sAtt m wD, Smaw, Tst bs, Hbst bg, qq, nbt, Hr nb
covered with green-malachite, southern, raise-up secret-image-of-god, clothes weary-one, devourer, mistress, upon any
'covered with southern Egyptian malachite, who raises up the secret image of the god, clothes the weary one, devourer, mistress of everyone'

rn n iry-aA.s, ir-sw-Ds.f
name of gate-keeper.its, made-he-himself
the name of its gate-keeper, Ir-su-djesef'

Ddwt xft spr, r sbxt, mHt-mdw, in Awsir Anwy, qAt-xrw

spoken-words when entering, to gateway, tenth, by Osiris Anwy, loud-voice

'Words to be spoke when entering the Tenth Gateway by Osiris Anwy, Qat-kheru'

nhsit qsnwt? sbt, nrw n SfSft.s

wake pain/misery/cries, laughter, fearsome of respect.her

'cries in misery and laughs, fearful of her respect'

nn snD.n.s, nty m Xnw.s, rn n iry-aA.s, s-xn-wr

not fear.of.she, who in within.it, name of gate-keeper.its, embrace-great

'She does not fear who is within it, the name of its gate-keeper, Sekhen-wer'

THE ELEVENTH GATEWAY (The following text: *Naville, Todtenbuch, Bd.I, B1, 11,12*)

sbxt mHt mdw-wa, wHmt dsw, wdbt sbiw, Hri n.s, sbxwt nbt

gateway eleventh, repeat knives, burner rebels, exorcise-ill of.she, gateways all

**'The Eleventh Gateway, repeating knives, burner of rebels,
she exorcises evil at all the gateways'**

irwt ihhy hrw, n ixxwt, iw.s, Xr sip, n Hbs bgA

making rejoicing day, of twilight, is.she, under inspection, of clothing weary-one/slack/remiss

'make rejoicing on the day of twilight, she is under inspection of clothing the slack one'

THE TWELTH GATEWAY

sbxt mHt-mdw-sn (12), nis tAwy.sy, sk iiw, m nhpw qAy

gateway twelfth, summon two-lands.its, wipe-out those-come, with early-morning bright-one?

**'The Twelfth Gateway, summons its two lands,
wiping out those who come in the early morning, and bright one'**

[hieroglyphs]

nbt Ax, sDmt nb.s, ra nb, iw.s, Xr sip

lady akh-spirits, hears lord.hers, day every, is.she, under inspection

'the Lady of Akh-spirits, she listens to her lord every day, she is under inspection'

[hieroglyphs]

n Hbst bgA

of clothing weary-one/slack/remiss

'of clothing the slack one'

THE THIRTEENTH GATEWAY

[hieroglyphs]

sbxt mHt-mdw-xmtw, sTA n ist, awy.s, Hr.s, s-HDt Hapy, m imnt.f

gateway thirteenth, drag/stretch of Isis, two-arms, over.it, make-bright Hapy, in secret-place.his

**'The Thirteenth Gateway, Isis has stretched her two arms over it,
making Hapy shine in his secret place'**

[hieroglyphs]
iw.s, Xr sipw, n Hbs, bgA
is.she, unde inspection, of clothing, weary-one/slack/remiss
'she is under inspection of clothing the limp one '

THE FOURTEENTH GATEWAY

[hieroglyphs]
sbxt mHt-mdw-fdw, nbt dsw, xbt Hr dSrw, iri.i, n.s
gateway fourteenth, lady wrath, dance upon blood, make.i, for.her
'The Fourteenth Gateway Lady of Wrath, who dances upon blood, I made for her'

[hieroglyphs]
hAk, hrw n sDm iw ·
Hak-god-festival, day of hearing injustice
'the festival of the god Hak on the day of hearing injustice'

(hieroglyphs)

iw.st, Xr sip, n Hbs bgA

is.she, inder inspection, of veiling slack/remiss

'she is under inspection of veiling the slack one'

THE FIFTEENTH GATEWAY

(hieroglyphs)

sbxt mHt-mdw-diw, bAyt, dSr, gmHwt iArrt, prt m grH

gateway fifteen, soul, red plaited-hair, weak-of-sight, come-forth by night

**'The Fifteenth Gateway, soul of the one of red plaited hair,
weak of sight coming forth by night'**

(hieroglyphs)

snDrt sbiw, Hr qAby.f, rdi awy.s, n wrd-ib

gasping rebels, upon belly.his, gives two-hands.her, for weary-heart

'who grasps the rebel by his belly and gives her two hands for the Weary One'

sbxt mHt-mdw-sisw, Dd mdw in, Awsir xft spr.f, r sbxt Tn

gateway sixteenth, spoken words by, Osiris when arriving.he, to gateway this

'The Sixteenth Gateway, words to be spoken when he arrives at this gateway'

nrwtt, nbt iAdt, xAa xAw m bA, n rmT

terrible-one, lady pestilence/rain-storm cast-away thousands from souls, of people

'the Terrible One, Lady of the Rainstorm, who casts away thousands of souls of the people'

xbsw mt, n rmT, srt pri, qmAmt

hacks-up dead, of mankind, decapitate? goes-out, who-creates

'who hacks up the dead of humankind, who decapitates those who come forth, who creates'

(hieroglyphs)
Sat, iw.s, Xr.s, sip n Hbs bgA
terror/blood-lust, is.she, under.she, examination of clothed weary-one
'blood-lust terror, she is under the examination of the clothed Weary One'

THE SEVENTEENTH GATEWAY

(hieroglyphs)
sbxt mHt-mdw-sfxw, xbt Hr snfw, iHy[...] nbt, wAwywAyt
gateway seventeenth, dances upon blood ...[...] lady fire
'The Seventeenth Gateway, she who dances upon blood ... Lady of Fire'

(hieroglyphs)
iw.s, Xr sip, n Hbs bgA
is.she, under inspection, of clothed weary-one
'she is holding an inspection of the clothed Weary One'

sbxt mHt-mdw-xmnw, mr stAw, wab iAbtw

gateway eighteenth, loves heat, purify brand-mark?

'The Eighteenth Gateway, lover of heat, purifier of brand marks'

---

mrr.s, Sad tpw, imAxyt nbt Hwt-a, wHst sbiw, mSrw

loves.she, cut-off heads, venerated lady mansion, kills rebels, in evening

'she loves to cut off heads, Venerated Lady of the Mansion, who kills rebels in the evening'

---

iw.s, Xr sip, n Hbs bgA

is.she, under inspection, of clothed weary-one

'she is holding an inspection of the clothed Weary One'

sbxt mHt-mdw-psDt, srt nhpw, m aHa.s, wrS Smmwt

gateway nineteenth, anounce dawn, in time.her, spend-time heating

'The Nineteenth Gateway, she anounces the dawn in her time and spends her time burning'

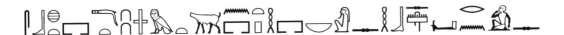

nbt wsrw, sSw n DHwty Ds.f, iw.s, xr sip.f, Hbsw n Sini

lady power, writings of Thoth self.him, is.she, holding inpection.his of treasury?

**'Lady of Power of the writings of Thoth himself,
She is under his supervision of the veiled ones of the Treasury'**

THE TWENTIETH GATEWAY

sbxt mHt-Dbaty, imt-Xnw, tpH nb.s, Hbs rn.s

gateway twentieth, who-within, cavern lord.her, veiled name.her

'The Twentieth Gateway, who is within the cavern of her lord, veiled is her name'

imnt qmAmw.s, Ttt HAtyw, qq mw.s
hidden created-forms.she, takes hearts, devours? water.she
'hidden she of created forms, who devours water'

iw.s, xr sip, Hbsw n Sini
is.she, holding inpection of treasury?
'she is under supervision of the veiled ones of the Treasury'

THE TWENTY-FIRST GATEWAY

sbxt mHt-Dbaty-wa, dm dsyA, r Ddw, ir Hmn
gateway twenty-first, sharp knife, against speaker, acts-as slayer
'The Twenty-First Gateway, sharp of knife who is against the speaker, who acts as slayer'

(hieroglyphs)
hAy nbiw.s, iw.s, Xr sxrw imn
descends flame.hers, is.she, under govenance secret
'who descends in her flame, she is under secret govenance'

PLATE 12: UTTERANCE 18

Top Register (left): Anwy and his wife Tutu are introduced to the gods by a Sem-Priest dressed in a leopard skin, Iwn-Mut-ef:

(hieroglyphs) **iwn-mwt-f** '(Horus) Pillar of His Mother'

Bottom Register (left): Anwy and his wife are introduced to the gods by Sem-priest Sa-mer-ef:

(hieroglyphs) **sA-mr.f** 'Son whom He Loves'

Register (Right): the seated gods: Temu, Shu, Tefnut, Osiris and Thoth
Register (Far Right): the seated gods: Osiris, Isis, Nephthys and Horus

(hieroglyphs)
dwA Awsir, nb r-sTAw, psDt nTrw aAt, imy Xrt-nTr, in Awsir sS Anwy
adoration Osiris, lord Rostjawu, Pesedet gods great, who-is-in necropolis, by Osiris scribe Anwy
'The adoration of Osiris, Lord of Rosetjau, and the Great Pesedet of gods, **who are in the God's Domain, by Osiris Scribe, Anwy'**

Dd.f, inD Hr.k, xnty imntt, wn-nfr Hr ib AbDw, iiy xr.k, ib.i, Xr mAat

says.he, homage upon.you, foremost west, Wenemnefer upon heart Abydos,
come before.you, heart.my, possessing truth

**'he says, homage to you, Foremost of the West, Wenemnefer dwelling in Abydos,
I come before you, my heart possessing truth'**

nn isf, m Xt.i, nn Dd grg, m rx, nn iry, sp-sn

not wrongdoing, in body.my, not say falsehood, with knowing, not done misdeed, repeat-twice

**'without wrongdoing in my body, without falsehood knowingly,
without doing misdeed, repeat twice'**

rdi.k, n.i, tAw, pr m-bAH, Hr xAwt, nbw mAat, ii aq Xrt-nTr

give.you, to.me, bread, come before upon altar, truth possessors, come-forth enter-in necropolis

**'may you give to me bread which comes in the presence of the altar of the possessors of truth,
may I come out and go in to the Necropolis'**

nn Sntw, bA.i, mAA iTn, dgg iaH, DtA sp-sn

not hindered ba.my, see Aten, espy moon forever, repeat-twice

**'may my Ba not be hindered, may I see the sun-disc (Aten)
and behold the moon forever, to be repeated twice'**

Dd in, iwn-mwt.f, Dd.f, iiy xr.tnw, wDAtDAw aAt, imyw pt tA Xrt-nTr

say by, Pillar-Mother.His, says.he, come.i under.you, councilors great,
who-are-in heaven earth necropolis

**'spoken by the Pillar-of-his-Mother, he says I have come before you great councilors,
who are in heaven, earth and the Necropolis'**

---

ini.n.i, n.tnw, Awsir Anwy, nn btA.f, xr nTr nbw

bring.of.i, to.you, Osiris Anwy, not wrong.he, under god all

'I bring to you, Osiris Anwy, who is blameless before all the gods'

(hieroglyphs)
imma wn.f, Hna.tnw, hrw nb
grant be.he, with.you, day every
'grant that he may be with you every day'

(hieroglyphs)
Dd mdw, sA mr.f, Dd.f, iiy xr.tnw, DAtDAw imyw r-sTAw
spoken words by, son bbeloved.his, says.he, come under.you, councillors lords who-in Rosetjau
'words to be spoken by the Son-whom-he-Loves, he says, **I come before you divine beings, lords of Rosetjau'**

(hieroglyphs)
ini.n, n.tnw, Awsir Anwy, imma tAw mw TAw, sAH m sxt-Htp
bring.of, to.you, Osiis Anwy, grant bread, water, breath, grant-of-land in field-offerings
'I have brought to you Osiris Anwy, may you grant bread, water and breath **and land in the Field of Offerings'**

𓎡𓏤𓅃𓀀
mi Smsw Hrw
like followers Horus
'like the followers of Horus'

sbA Awsir, nb DtA, DAtDAw nbw r-stAw, in wsir [Anwy], Dd.f, inD Hr.k, nswt Xrt-nTr
adoration Osiris, lord eternity, counsilors all Rosetjau, by Osiris, says.he, homage upon.you, king god's-domain
'The adoration of Osiris, Lord of Eternity and all the councilors of Rosetjau, by the Osiris [Scribe Anwy], he says homage to you king of the God's Domain'

𓃀𓏤𓊨𓀀𓆓𓏏𓀭𓈖𓇋𓎼𓂋𓂋𓏏𓈇𓇋𓇋𓂻𓐍𓂋𓎡𓂋𓐍𓎡𓋴𓐍𓂋𓅱𓎡𓂝𓊪𓂋𓎡𓅓𓇋𓂋𓅱𓎡𓈖𓇼𓇳
HqA nw igrrt, iiy xr.k, rx.k, sxrw.k, apr.k, m irw.k, n dwAt
prince of silent-land, know.you, plans.your, equip.you, with forms.your, of underworld
'Ruler of the Silent Land, you know your plans, you equip with your forms of the Underworld'

rdi.k, n.i, st m Xrt-nTr, rmA nbw mAat, sAH.i, mn m sxt-Htpw

give.you, to.i, place in god's-domain, in-presence lords truth, equip.i established in field-offerings

'may you give to me a place in the God's Domain and in the presence of the Lords of Truth, may I be equipped with establishment in the Field of Offerings'

sSp snw m-bAH.k

receive offerings before.you

'may I receive offerings in your presence'

PLATE 13: Utterance 18 (Continued)

i DHwty, s-mAa-xrw Awsir, r xftyw.f, s-mAa-xrw Awsir, r xftyw.f

hail Thoth, make-victorious Osiris, against enemies.his, make-victorious Osiris, against enemies.his

'Hail Thoth who makes Osiris victorious against his enemies, who makes Osiris (Anwy) victorious aginst his enemies'

mi s-mAa-xrw Awsir, r xftyw.f, m-bAH DADAwt, imt ra, imt Awsir

like making-victorious Osiris, against enemies.his, in-presence magistrates,
who-with Ra, who-with Osiris

**'like making Osiris victorious against his enemies in the presence of the judging-magistrates
who are with Ra and Osiris'**

---

imt iwnnw, grH n xt xAwy, grH pwy, n aHA

who-in Heliopolis, night of things night, night that, of fighting

'who were in Heliopolis on the night of things of the night, that night of fighting'

---

a, n irt sAwt, sbiw hrw pw, n Htm.tw

condition/state, of doing guarding, rebels day that, of destroying

'at the time of guarding the rebels on that day of destroying'

[hieroglyphs]
xftyw nw nb-r-Dr
enemies of Neb-er-Djer
'the enemies of the Lord-of-All'

[hieroglyphs]
ir DADAwt aA, imt iwnnw, tmw pw, Sw pw, tfnwt pw
as-to magistrates great, who-in Heliopolis, Temu it-is, Shu it-is, Tefnut it-is
'as to the Great Judges who are in Heliopolis, they are Temu, Shu and Tefnut'

[hieroglyphs]
ir sAyw sbiw, Htm.n.tw, smAyw
as-to guardians rebels, destruction.of.one, companions
'as to regarding the guardians of the rebels, it is the destruction of the companions'

<table>
<tr><td>

[hieroglyphs]

</td></tr>
<tr><td>

st pw, m wHm, qn.tw.f

</td></tr>
<tr><td>

Seth it-is, as repeat, evil.one.his

</td></tr>
<tr><td>

'of Seth when he repeated his evil'

</td></tr>
</table>

<table>
<tr><td>

[hieroglyphs]

</td></tr>
<tr><td>

i DHwty, s-mAa-xrw Awsir, r xftyw.f, s-mAa-xrw Osiris Anwy

</td></tr>
<tr><td>

hail Thoth, made-victorious Osiris, against enemies.his, made-victorious Osiris Anwy

</td></tr>
<tr><td>

'hail Thoth, made victorious against his enemies, made victorious, Osiris Anwy'

</td></tr>
</table>

<table>
<tr><td>

[hieroglyphs]

</td></tr>
<tr><td>

Anwy r xftyw.f, m DADAwt aAt, imt Ddw

</td></tr>
<tr><td>

Anwy against enemies.his, before magistrates great, who-in Busiris

</td></tr>
<tr><td>

'Anwy, made victorious against his enemies before the great magistrates who are in Busiris'

</td></tr>
</table>

 𓊪𓈎𓏏𓉾𓂧𓏲𓇋𓇋𓈖𓋴𓂝𓉻𓏏𓊽𓅓𓊽𓊽𓅆
grH pwy, n s-aHa Dd, m Ddw
night that, of making-stand Djed-pillar, in Busiris
'on that night of standing erect the Djed-Pillar (of Osiris) in Busiris'

 𓇋𓇋𓇋𓇯𓂧𓂧𓄿𓅱𓏏𓂝𓂝𓏏𓊽𓊽𓅆𓇋𓅓𓏏𓊽𓊽𓅆𓁹𓊨𓅆𓊨𓏏𓅆𓎟𓉗𓏏𓅆
ir DADAwt aAt, imt Ddw, Awsir pw, ist pw, nb-Hwt pw
as-to magistrates great, who-in Busiris, Osiris it-is, Isis it-is, Nephthys it-is
'as to the magistrates who are in Busiris, it is Osiris, it is Isis, it is Nephthys'

 𓅂𓅱𓅆𓄤𓁷𓏏𓆑𓇋𓂋𓋴𓂝𓉾𓊽𓅓𓊽𓊽𓅆�qaH𓅱𓈖𓅃𓅆
Hrw pw, nD Hr it, ir s-aHa Dd, m Ddw, qaH pw, n Hrw
Horus it-is, avenger upon father, as-to making-stand ded-pillar, in Busiris, shoulder it-is, of Horus'
'it is Horus, the Avenger of His Father, as to making erect the Pillar of Osiris, it is the shoulder of Horus'

xnty xm, iw.snw, HA-tp Awsir, m mrw, n Hbsw

foremost Letopolis, are.they, behind Osiris, in binding, of cloth

'Foremost of Letopolis, they are behind Osiris in the binding of cloth'

i DHwty, s-mAa-xrw, r xftyw.f, s-mAa-xrw Awsir Anwy, mAa-xrw

hail Thoth, make-victorious, against enemies.his, make-victorious Osiris Anwy, true-voice

'Hail Thoth made victorious against his enemies,
made victorious Osiris Anwy, True of Voice'

wDA judge, litigate, judged, weighed in judgement

abreviation for: **s-rs causative:** awaken, watch, guard, vigilant, take command **wTst:** post (of balance); **wTs:** raise, lift, carry, wear;

wTs-tp vigilant, watchful

arywt portal/door/gate/dwelling

, , , **iry-aA** door-keeper

iry-at hall-keeper

sAw guardian (noun); guard/ward-off/retrain (verb)

, **sAwty, sAyt** guardian

smi announcer

xsf drive away, ward off, oppose, **repel**, repress crime, redress wrong, punishment, disaproval, **punish**, reprove words, drive cattle, divert water, avoid anger, prevent

rs 'indeed'

nm 'who?'

xrt 'state, condition, affairs, concerns, requirements, products of a place'

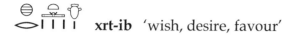 **xrt-ib** 'wish, desire, favour'

Xr 'under, carrying, holding, possessing, at head or foot, through of means, subject to someone's actions'

Dr 'end, since, before, until'

ntt 'that'

nty 'that, which, who?'

wn mAa 'true being, reality, true-right'

aHa 'stand, stand by, stand erect, raise oneself, stand up, rise up, arise, attend, wait, lifetime'

sp 'time, period, times, twice, matter, affair, deed, act, misdeed, fault, occasion, chance, venture, success'; note: **spt** 'threshing floor'

Hr face, sight; (prepostion with suffixes) 'upon, in, at, from, on account of, concerning, through, and, having on it, because'

Hr-awy 'immediately'

Hr-m 'why?'

Hr-sA 'upon, outside, after, in turn'

ti phonetic sound **ti,** enclitic particle: 'yes, yeah'; 'lo, you, yours, hers'

ti phonetic sound **ti,** enclitic particle: 'yes, yeah'; 'lo, you, yours, hers'

aHa.n introduces narrative past tense: 'pay attention to this, listen to this'

tr 'forsooth, pray'

A enclitic particle, with exclamatory force 'A!'

nA 'this, these, here, the, hither'

ist 'lo'

rf 'now, then'

iry 'thereof, thereto'

ir 'as to, if'

iry 'thereof, thereto'

tw 'you, your, one, this, that'

is 'after all, indeed, even, in fact'

iw 'is, are, behold' starts a sentence

tp-Hsb 'reckoning, standard, rectitude (high moral standard)' lit. in front of reckoning

pw 'It is, They are, this, who? what? whichever?'

ix 'then, therefore, what?'

xr non enclitic particle: 'and, further'; auxillary verb: 'so says'; preposition: 'with, near, under (a king), speak (to), by (of agent)'

rk 'but, now'

xft (preposition) 'in front of, in accordance with, as well as, corresponding to'; when, according to, at the time of, when, (speech) to (someone)

m-a preposition: 'in the hand, possession, charge of, together with, from'

Note: **m** enclitic particle (not translated); 'behold'; preposition 'in the hand, possession, charge of, together with, from'; imperative 'take'; interogative 'who, what'

bnw heron, 'Phoenix'

var. **baHi/baHw** heron on a perch (mound?), 'flood, be inundated, inundation'

baHw 'flood, inundation'

baH 'inundated land'

baH 'abundance'

The Ogdoad

NU + NUANET

AMUN + AMAUNET   KUK +KAUKET   HUH + HAUET

Osiris was the son of Nut and Seb (Hymn to Osiris, Papyrus of Anwy)

Osiris was the son of Ra or Geb (Gebeb, Kebeb, Seb, Keb, Earth god) and his mother was Nut (Ennead of Heliopolis).

Nu and Nut were brother-sister and husband-wife.

The eight deities were arranged in four male-female pairs: Nu and Naunet, Amun and Amaunet, Kuk and Kauket, Huh and Hauhet. The males were associated with frogs and females were associated with snakes.[1] Apart from their gender, there was little to distinguish the male gods and female goddesses; indeed, the names of the females are merely derivative female forms of the male name. Essentially, each pair represents the male and female aspect of one of four concepts, namely the primordial waters (Nu and Naunet), air or invisibility (Amun and Amaunet), darkness (Kuk and Kauket), and eternity or infinity (Huh and Hauhet).

Together the four concepts represent the primal, fundamental state of the beginning. They are what always was. In the myth, however, their interaction ultimately proved to be unbalanced, resulting in the arising of a new entity. When the entity opened, it revealed Ra, the fiery sun, inside. After a long interval of rest, Ra, together with the other deities, created all other things.

The entity containing Ra is depicted either as an egg or as a lotus bud.

In the former version, a mound arises from the waters. An egg was laid upon this mound by a celestial bird. The egg contained Ra. In some variants, the egg is laid by a cosmic goose. However, the egg was also said to have been a gift from Thoth, and laid by an ibis, the bird with which he was associated.

Later, when Atum had become assimilated into Ra as Atum-Ra, the belief that Atum emerged from a (blue) lotus bud, in the Ennead cosmogony, was adopted and attached to Ra. The lotus was said to have arisen from the waters after the explosive interaction as a bud, which floated on the surface, and slowly opened its petals to reveal the beetle, Khepri, inside. Khepri, an aspect of Ra representing the rising sun, immediately turns into a weeping boy – Nefertum, whose tears form the creatures of the earth.

The Ennead

ATUM

SHU + TEFNUT

GEB + NUT

OSIRIS + ISIS (SISTER + WIFE)   SETH + NEPHTHYS

HORUS   ANUBIS

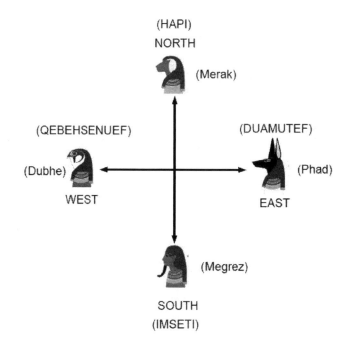

(HAPI)
NORTH
(Merak)

(QEBEHSENUEF)   (DUAMUTEF)

(Dubhe)   (Phad)

WEST   EAST

(Megrez)

SOUTH
(IMSETI)

The Imperishable/Indestructable Circumpolar Stars

The Indestructibles: Egyptian ikhemu-sek, 'the ones not knowing destruction,' was the name given by Ancient Egyptian astronomers to two bright stars which, at that time, could always be seen circling the North Pole. The name is directly related to Egyptian belief in constant North as a portal to heaven for pharaohs, and the stars' close association with eternity and the afterlife. These circumpolar stars are now known as **Kochab** (Beta Ursae Minoris), in the bowl of Ursa Minor or, the Little Dipper, and **Mizar** (Zeta Ursae Majoris), in Ursa Major, at the middle of the handle of the Big Dipper.

𓇳𓆣𓏏𓋴𓏏𓏤𓇼, 𓇳𓆣𓏏𓋴𓏤𓇼 **ixmw-sk** 'the indestructable star, the circumpolar star'

𓇳𓆣𓏏𓏤𓏤𓋴𓏤𓇼𓏤𓏤𓏤 **ixmw-skw** 'the indestructable stars'

𓇳𓏏𓏤𓏤𓏤𓆣𓏤𓏤𓇼𓏤𓏤𓏤 **ixmw-wrdw** 'the unwearying stars'

𓉆𓋹𓂝𓏜𓉐𓎆𓇳𓎡

'May you be given: Life - Prosperity - Health, Forever and Ever'

Kemet Scribe

http://arkpublishing.co.uk